宮沢賢治
原文英訳シリーズ3

『風の又三郎』
を英語で読む

収録作品
『風の又三郎』
『雪渡り』
『よだかの星』
『永訣の朝』

コスモピア

はじめに

永遠に輝き続ける光

　日本人がこの「奇想天外な児童書を書く風変わりな作家」を見直すようになったのは、1995年1月の阪神大震災とその2ヵ月後に東京で発生した地下鉄サリン事件の後のことです。バブル経済はその数年前に崩壊していました。それ自体が目的のように見えた明治時代の領土拡大モデルも、戦後の高度経済成長モデルも、悪く言えば、高いコストを伴う誤算であり、控えめに言っても、将来の計画に深刻な欠陥があったことがわかっています。日本人は今、自問しています。「わが国は、本当に私たちの福祉と幸福のために行動しているのだろうか？」と。

　2011年3月11日、東北地方で地震、津波、福島第一原子力発電所のメルトダウンという3つの災害が起きました。日本人はそのとき、バブル経済がはじけたさらに20年前の、混乱の極みに陥ったとき以上の暗い深淵に突き落とされたのです。私たちはどこへ行くのだろう？　どうすれば喜びと希望をもって自分の人生を生きられるのか？　他の人々に積極的な変化をもたらすことは可能なのだろうか？

　すべての人にとってより良い人生を創造する方法は何か？　その答えの鍵は、私たちを結びつけるものにあります。それは地球の自然です。

　この巻に収められている4つの作品ですが、すべて、光、風、空気、雪を媒介として生み出されています。賢治が死の床にある妹のトシに届けた雪は、空の彼方から贈られてきたものであり、トシ自身もいつの日か雪となり、その姿で地球に帰ってきます。よだかもまた、自然の別の側面である光を放つ星へと姿を変えます。『雪渡り』に登場するふたりの子どもは、文字通り動物たちが生き方を教えてくれる別世界へと渡っていきます。雪そのものが、モラルの伝達を可能にする媒体なのです。

そして、あの謎めいたキャラクター、風の又三郎こと高田三郎です。彼は風そのものを擬人化したような存在です。それゆえにポジティブな結果もネガティブな結果ももたらすことができます。風には家や傘などを破壊するネガティブな側面もあれば、風車のはたらきを可能にするようなポジティブな側面もあります。しかし、賢治にとっての風は、人間と自然とのコミュニケーションの媒体でもあります。自然は、これまで存在したすべての人間、そしてすべての動物や植物の生命を包みこんでいます。

　私たち人間は、地球の未来が、今まさに、私たちの目の前にあり、私たちの足元や頭上に存在しているという事実を受け入れたように思えます。したがって、木を切って材木を得たり、食料として動物を殺すといったような、最も単純な行動から、山を削ったり、化石燃料を使った発電所を建設するなどのより複雑な行動にいたるまで、今日、私たちが取るあらゆる行動、さらには呼吸、歩み、手に触れるすべての物が、地球の未来に影響を与えることを認識しなければなりません。

　この巻に収められた作品は、すべての生き物と生と死の謎に関わる倫理観を語っています。寛容、感情移入、愛こそが、現世で私たちを支え、一人ひとりが放つ光が永遠に輝き続けることを保証するのです。

　しかし、寛容、感情移入、愛は、人間が独自に作り出した真空の中には存在しません。寛容、感情移入、愛は、人間が地球の本質を深く理解するという相互作業を通してのみ存在するのです。

　生涯、自然科学に心酔していた宮沢賢治ほど、このことを深く理解していた日本人はいません。世界の人々もそれを知る必要があるでしょう。

2023年6月

ロジャー・パルバース

Roger Pulvers

目次

2	はじめに
6	音声ダウンロードの方法
7	音声ファイル表
8	電子版の使い方
9	宮沢賢治　略年譜

10 『風の又三郎』
The Boy of the Winds

読むまえに――
浮いた存在？ 変わり者？
オタク？ マニア？ 異邦人？

2学期が始まる9月1日の朝、教室にやってきた子どもたちは、不思議な赤毛の少年がいるのに気づく。

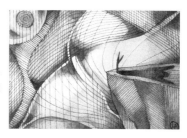

14 | 本編

116 『雪渡り』
Snow Crossing

読むまえに――
狐に包まれた人間たち

ある日、小狐の紺三郎と知り合った四郎とかん子の兄妹は、狐の小学校の幻燈会に誘われて……。

120 | 本編

イラスト：ルーシー・バルバース

154 『よだかの星』
The Nighthawk Star

読むまえに――
ひかりはたもたれ、電燈は失われ

よだかは鷹からはいじめられ、星たちからも蔑まれ、周りから常に冷たい扱いをうける。しかし、よだかは星になろうと決意した。そして死に物狂いで、自力で天上を目指していく……。

158 本編

176 『永訣の朝』
The Morning of Last Farewell

読むまえに――
天上のアイスクリーム

最愛の妹トシとの別れが刻々と迫ってくる。最期の時を迎えようとする中、賢治は空から降ってくるみぞれをお椀で受け止めようとする。その雪が妹の最後の食べ物になるのだ。賢治は深い悲しみと慟哭の果てに何を見るのか。

180 本編

本書の宮沢賢治の原作はちくま文庫の「宮沢賢治全集」を底本としています。
その上で、『風の又三郎』『雪渡り』『よだかの星』の3編については新仮名遣いに変更するとともに一部の漢字を改めています。
韻文である『永訣の朝』に関しては、底本のまま旧仮名遣いで掲載しています。

音声ダウンロードの方法

音声をスマートフォンやPCで、簡単に聞くことができます。

方法1 スマホで聞く場合

面倒な手続きなしにストリーミング再生で聞くことができます。

※ストリーミング再生になりますので、通信制限などにご注意ください。
　また、インターネット環境がない状況でのオフライン再生はできません。

このサイトにアクセスするだけ！

https://soundcloud.com/yqgfmv3ztp15/
sets/tbav1gtp203k

❶ 上記サイトに**アクセス！**

❷ アプリを使う場合は SoundCloud に アカウント登録（無料）

方法2 パソコンで音声ダウンロードする場合

パソコンで mp3 音声をダウンロードして、スマホなどに取り込むことも可能です。

（スマホなどへの取り込み方法はデバイスによって異なります）

❶ 下記のサイトにアクセス

https://www.cosmopier.com/
download/4864541985

❷ 中央のボタンをクリックする

音声は PC の一括ダウンロード用圧縮ファイル（ZIP 形式）でご提供します。
解凍してお使いください。

音声ファイル表

File No.		
1	*p.*10	**The Boy of the Winds**
	*p.*14	1 September
2	*p.*34	2 September
3	*p.*46	Sunday, 4 September
4	*p.*72	5 September
5	*p.*84	7 September
6	*p.*96	8 September
7	*p.*108	12 September, Day Twelve
8	*p.*116	**Snow Crossing**
	*p.*120	Part One Konzaburo the Little Fox
9	*p.*136	Part Two Magic Lantern Party at the Fox Elementary School
10	*p.*154/158	**The Nighthawk Star**
11	*p.*180	**The Morning of Last Farewell**

タイトルと本文は同じ音声ファイルの中に収録されています。

電子版の使い方

音声ダウンロード不要
ワンクリックで音声再生！

本書購読者は
無料でご使用いただけます！
音声付きで
本書がそのままスマホでも
読めます。

電子版ダウンロードには
クーポンコードが必要です

詳しい手順は下記をご覧ください。
右下の QR コードからもアクセスが
可能です。

電子版：無料引き換えコード
Q8t3Rt

ブラウザベース（HTML5 形式）でご利用
いただけます。

★クラウドサーカス社 ActiBook 電子書籍
　（音声付き）です。

●対応機種
・PC（Windows/Mac）　・iOS（iPhone/iPad）
・Android（タブレット、スマートフォン）

電子版ご利用の手順

❶コスモピア・オンラインショップにアクセス
　してください。（無料ですが、会員登録が必要です）

https://www.cosmopier.net/

❷ログイン後、カテゴリ「電子版」のサブカテゴリ「書籍」をクリックして
　ください。

❸本書のタイトルをクリックし、「カートに入れる」をクリックしてください。

❹「カートへ進む」→「レジに進む」と進み、「クーポンを変更する」をクリック。

❺「クーポン」欄に本ページにある無料引き換えコードを入力し、「登録する」を
　クリックしてください。

❻０円になったのを確認して、「注文する」をクリックしてください。

❼ご注文を完了すると、「マイページ」に電子書籍が登録されます。

宮沢賢治　略年譜

1896年　〈明治29年〉8月　岩手県現在の花巻市に生まれる

1909年　（明治42年）4月、岩手県立盛岡中学校に入学

1914年　（大正3年）3月、盛岡中学卒業

1915年　（大正4年）4月、盛岡高等農林学校入学

1917年　（大正6年）同人誌『アザリア』を発行

1918年　（大正7年）農学校を卒業。研究生として残る

1920年　（大正9年）5月、農林学校研究生を卒業。法華宗系在家仏教団
　　　　体、国柱会に入信

1921年　（大正10年）東京に出奔するも地元に戻り、稗貫郡立稗貫農学
　　　　校（翌年、花巻農学校に）の教諭に。この頃、『よだかの星』
　　　　を執筆。12月と翌年1月に『雪渡り』が『愛国婦人』誌に掲載。
　　　　生前に手にした唯一の原稿料。

1922年　（大正11年）11月27日妹のトシ死去。『永訣の朝』

1924年　（大正13年）『春と修羅』を自費出版。『銀河鉄道の夜』に着手。
　　　　短編集『注文の多い料理店』を刊行

1926年　（大正15年）花巻農学校を依願退職。その後も農業指導などに
　　　　関わる。チェロを購入

1928年　（昭和3年）肺浸潤の診断をうける。その後、一時回復するも
　　　　病臥生活に

1931年　（昭和6年）『雨ニモマケズ』

1932年　（昭和7年）『児童文学』2号に『グスコーブドリの伝記』を発表

1933年　〈昭和8年〉9月21日死去

1934年　（昭和9年）死後、『銀河鉄道の夜』刊行、『セロ弾きのゴーシュ』
　　　　『風の又三郎』『よだかの星』発表

風の又三郎
The Boy of the Winds

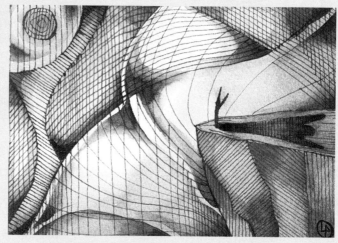

イラスト：ルーシー・バルバース

🔊 1-7

1: *p*.10 / *p*.14 1 September

2: *p*.34 2 September

3: *p*.46 Sunday, 4 September

4: *p*.72 5 September

5: *p*.84 7 September

6: *p*.96 8 September

7: *p*.108 12 September, Day Twelve

The Boy of the Winds を読むまえに

浮いた存在？ 変わり者？ オタク？ マニア？ 異邦人？

2学期が始まる9月1日の朝、教室にやってきた子どもたちは赤毛の少年がいるのに気づいた。転校生の高田三郎だ。不思議な能力をもち「又三郎」と呼ばれる少年は……

どっどど　どどうど　どどうど　どどう、

青いくるみも吹きとばせ

すっぱいかりんもふきとばせ

どっどど　どどうど　どどうど　どどう

　これは『風の又三郎』の有名な冒頭の言葉です。賢治が風のうなりの
ようなオノマトペによってこの物語を始めるのは自然なことです。風は
万物を動かします。風が音楽を奏で、それに合わせて私たちは人生のダ
ンスを踊ります。第1巻と第2巻の解説で述べたことの繰り返しになり
ますが、賢治の言葉のイメージは、日本の詩人が何世紀にもわたって使っ
てきたような日本の四季を描写するものではありません。賢治の言葉は
現実を新たな次元へと引き上げるものです。その次元から、私たちは地
球上、そして宇宙における自分の居場所を見ることができます。そのメッ
セージを運んでくれるのが風なのです。過去からの風は、良いことも悪
いことも含めて、未来に転化する予兆を含んでいます。

　『風の又三郎』は、賢治の他の作品と同様、それなりに道徳的な物語で
すが、宗教的な内容はほとんどなく、明確で直線的な親しみやすい物語
です。「風の三郎」とは、東北と北陸にわたって吹く風の名前です。この
風が最も強く吹くのは、旧暦の立春から数えて二百十日目、年によって
違うのですが、8月31日から9月2日の間です。これは台風シーズン
にほぼ一致します。風は10日間続くと言われ、又三郎が青空に舞い戻
るのはそのあとです。

　突然やってきた又三郎。教室で彼を見つけた瞬間から、地元の子ども
たちは皆、又三郎に惹きつけられます。彼はおとなしく、集団行動には
なかなかなじめない少年のようです。子どもたちはすぐに又三郎の超能

力に気がつきます。又三郎は子どもたちの嫉妬の対象であると同時に嘲笑の対象にもなります。ガラスのマントと赤い髪を持つ又三郎は、間違いなく普通の日本人ではなく別世界の人間です。賢治の作品の登場人物には外国人の名前が多いのですが、この物語に出てくる名前は日本風でもあり、田舎風でもあります。この男の子の名前にある「又」は「ふたたび」という意味で、風の姿をした又三郎が様々な場所を頻繁に訪れ、前に来た何かの生まれ変わりのようなものであることを示しています。彼は標準語を話しますが、少年たちは地元の東北弁を使う。又三郎は洋服を着て靴を履き、少年たちは和服の下に腰布を身につけ、下駄を履いています。

　賢治がこの物語を書くきっかけとなったのは、種山ヶ原を訪れたときだと言われています。 種山ヶ原は標高600メートルから870メートルの高原です。賢治の故郷である花巻の南東55キロに位置し、生まれ故郷の岩手県で賢治のお気に入りの場所のひとつでした。彼の作品のいくつかは、この地の風景からインスピレーションを得て作られています。

　私は2011年10月に種山ヶ原に行き、そこで何時間も過ごしました（賢治と東日本大震災をテーマにした4部構成のNHKのテレビシリーズを撮影するためでした）。賢治の物語に登場するアザミ、すすき、笹が、賢治の時代と同じようにそこにありました。種山ヶ原に広がる草原は広大で、空まで続いていました。手のひらを伸ばせば空に触れられそうなほど、空を近くに感じた場所は初めてでした。その日は風は強くなかったのですが、平原を駆け抜ける風は恐ろしいと言われています。

　『風の又三郎』は、宮沢賢治の物語として初めて映画化されたものです。大手映画会社の日活が1940年に東京の玉川撮影所で映画化し、賢治の

死から 7 年後の 10 月 10 日に公開されました。モノクロで 97 分。私は
この映画を見たことがありますが、原作とそのテーマを魅力的かつ忠実
に表現しているものでした。三郎を演じた片山明彦は撮影当時 13 歳。
その後、数十本の映画やテレビドラマに出演し、2014 年に 88 歳でこの
世を去りました。

　賢治の物語や詩には数え切れないほどの風が吹いています。亡くなる
数年前、療養中に書かれた「風がおもてで呼んでゐる」という詩では、
外で大きな風が自分を呼んでいるのが聞こえます。その風は、あの世か
ら賢治に、「『……うつくしいソプラノをもった／おれたちなかのひとり
と／約束通り結婚しろ』と繰り返し繰り返し……叫んでいる」。自然は彼
の恋人であり、その恋人と永遠の抱擁を交わしたとき、彼は真の意味で
自然の一部となるのです。

　私がこの『風の又三郎』という物語を愛するのは、賢治の地元を舞台
にしたその美しさと、人間と自然を融合させる力を持つ風を擬人化して
いる点からです。もう 50 年以上も前のことですが、賢治の弟の清六さん
から、賢治は、風を、自分の命という炎を吹き消し、その命を次の世界
へと運ぶ媒体として語っていた、と聞いたことがありました。

　宮沢賢治ほど、子どもの心の内面を忠実に、丹念に再現した日本人作
家はいないと思います。作家であり、劇作家であり、私の無二の親友で
ある井上ひさしは、かつて私にこう言いました。「宮沢賢治には不純物が
ない」。言い換えれば、世の中には憎しみ、罪深さ、残忍な不義があふれ
ていますが、賢治の中にはそれを克服し、より優しく、より思いやりの
ある自分になろうとする純粋な志があるのです。

1 September

Howl and thunder … howl roar HOWL!
Wind, blow off the fresh-green walnuts
Wind, blow off the sour quinces
Howl and thunder … howl roar HOWL!

A little school was located by a riverbank in a ravine.

It consisted of a single classroom for pupils from grades one to six. The yard was only about as big as a tennis court with a grotto in one corner that spurted out ice-cold water. There was also a beautiful mountain right behind the yard covered in grasses and weeds and dotted with chestnut trees.

On the invigorating morning of the first of September the wind was howling in the blue sky and the yard was bathed in sunlight. Two first-grade pupils came around from the embankment into the yard dressed in heavy black work pants.

"Wow, we're the first ones in … the first!" they shouted, very pleased with themselves, as they passed through the school gate. But they were stopped dead in their tracks when they peered with alarm into the classroom. They stared at each other, trembling and quaking. One of them burst into tears. The reason for this outburst was a funny red-haired boy that they didn't recognize sitting up at the desk in the front row of the otherwise empty room. And if this wasn't the desk where the boy who was bawling always sat!

The other boy was on the verge of tears too but forced himself to keep his eyes peeled on the new boy when he heard someone yelling from upriver.

九月一日

どっどど　どどうど　どどうど　どどう、
青いくるみも吹きとばせ
すっぱいかりんもふきとばせ
どっどど　どどうど　どどうど　どどう

＊以下、語注の訳の「　」の部分は原作からの引用です。英文と原作の意味がそのまま対応している部分になります。

Howl　（風などが）うなる

Fresh-green walnuts「青いくるみ」

quinces「かりん」

ravine　渓谷

pupils「生徒」

grotto「岩穴」、洞窟

spurted out「噴く」、噴き出す

dotted with...　〜が点在した、〜が散在した

chestnut trees「栗の木」

invigorating「さわやかな」、活気づける

embankment「どて」

work pants「雪袴」

stopped dead in their tracks「棒立ちになり」、突然止まる

bawling　（大声で）「泣く」

keep his eyes peeled on「目をりんと張って」、目をひんむいて、目をこらして

谷川の岸に小さな学校がありました。

教室はたった一つでしたが生徒は一年から六年までみんなありました。運動場もテニスコートのくらいでしたがすぐうしろは栗の木のあるきれいな草の山でしたし、運動場の隅にはごぼごぼつめたい水を噴く岩穴もあったのです。

さわやかな九月一日の朝でした。青ぞらで風がどうと鳴り、日光は運動場いっぱいでした。黒い雪袴をはいた二人の一年生の子がどてをまわって運動場にはいって来て、まだほかに誰も来ていないのを見て

「ほう、おら一等だぞ。一等だぞ。」とかわるがわる叫びながら大悦びで門をはいって来たのでしたが、ちょっと教室の中を見ますと、二人ともまるでびっくりして棒立ちになり、それから顔を見合せてぶるぶるふるえました。がひとりはとうとう泣き出してしまいました。というわけは、そのしんとした朝の教室のなかにどこから来たのか、まるで顔も知らないおかしな赤い髪の子供がひとり一番前の机にちゃんと座っていたのです。そしてその机といったらまったくこの泣いた子の自分の机だったのです。もひとりの子ももう半分泣きかけていましたが、それでもむりやり眼をりんと張ってそっちのほうをにらめていましたら、ちょうどそのとき川上から

"Caw-rattle-coo-click! Caw-rattle-coo-click!"

Kasuke, smiling a toothy smile and clutching his school bag, came flying into the yard like an enormous crow, followed hot on his heels by the likes of Sataro and Kosuke.

"What ya blubberin' about, crybaby?" said Kasuke, grabbing the shoulder of the boy who was doing his best to hold back his tears. "You stickin' yer nose in where it don't belong?" This caused the boy to snivel and sob. All the boys looked into the classroom and saw the weird little redhead boy sitting up straight as a pin at the desk. They all fell silent. The girls arrived, one after another, joining them … and there wasn't a peep out of any of them.

The redhead boy was as calm as a cucumber as he sat very properly at the desk, staring at the blackboard. That's when Ichiro, who was in the sixth grade, showed up.

"What's goin' on?" he said to the others, striding at a leisurely pace, just like an adult, to where they were milling about.

They all babbled at the same time, pointing to the weird boy in the classroom. Ichiro, holding his school bag to his chest, rushed to a window and stood below it. All the others felt the urge to follow him.

"Who would dare to go to class before it's time to, eh?" said Ichiro, as he crept up the wall and poked his face in the window.

"Anyone who goes inside early on a nice day like this'll get the book thrown at 'em by the teacher!" said Kosuke from below.

"It's no skin off my back if some kid gets in the teacher's bad books," said Kasuke.

Caw-rattle-coo-click! 「ちょうはあかぐり」。原文には諸説あるが、嘉助が「まるで大きなからすのように」かけてきたとあることから、鳥の鳴き声を用いた語呂合わせとなっている。caw はカーというカラスの鳴き声で、rattle はガラガラという音や子どもの玩具のラトル

hot on his heels 「すぐそのあとから」

the likes of... （のような）人たち

blubberin' 泣きじゃくる、泣きわめく

You stickin' yer nose in where it don't belong? 「うなかもたのが」。原文は、東北の方言で「お前がちょっかい出したのか」という意味を持つ（Stick one's nose where it doesn't belong: 余計な詮索をする、ちょっかいをだす）

sitting up straight as a pin 「しゃんとすわって」

There wasn't a peep out of any of them 「誰もなんとも言えませんでした」

striding at a leisurely pace 「大股にやってきて」

milling about （群衆などが）ひしめく

babbled 「がやがや」（話す）

get the book thrown at... 「うんと叱られる」、〜を厳しく罰する

no skin off my back 「知らない」

「ちょうはあかぐり　ちょうはあかぐり」と高く叫ぶ声がしてそれからまるで大きな鳥のように嘉助が、かばんをかかえてわらって運動場へかけて来ました。と思ったらすぐそのあとから佐太郎だの耕助だのやどややってきました。

「なして泣いでら、うなかもたのが。」嘉助が泣かないこどもの肩をつかまえて言いました。するとその子もわあと泣いてしまいました。おかしいとおもってみんながあたりを見ると教室の中にあの赤毛のおかしな子がすましてしゃんとすわっているのが目につきました。みんなはしんとなってしまいました。だんだんみんな女の子たちも集って来ましたが誰もなんとも言えませんでした。

赤毛の子どもは一向こわがる風もなくやっぱりちゃんと座ってじっと黒板を見ています。

すると六年生の一郎が来ました。一郎はまるでおとなのようにゆっくり大股にやってきてみんなを見て「何した」とききました。みんなははじめてがやがや声をたててその教室の中の変な子を指しました。一郎はしばらくそっちを見ていましたがやがて鞄をしっかりかかえてさっさと窓の下へ行きました。

みんなもすっかり元気になってついて行きました。

「誰だ、時間にならないに教室へはいってるのは。」一郎は窓へはいのぼって教室の中へ顔をつき出して言いました。

「お天気のいい時教室さ入ってるづど先生にうんと叱らえるぞ。」窓の下の耕助が言いました。

「叱らえでもおら知らないよ。」嘉助が言いました。

"Get outta that room! Get outta that room right now!" cried Ichiro.

But the boy in the classroom just looked in their direction as if a bit startled, sitting with his hands primly on his knees.

The boy's demeanor was, in a word, bizarre. He wore a weird gray baggy jacket, white short pants and low red leather shoes without an ankle strap. As for his face, it looked like a ripe apple, and his googly eyes were jet black. He didn't seem to understand what they were all saying, and this left Ichiro entirely stumped.

"The guy's a foreigner!"

"This must be his first day."

They all jabbered away until Kasuke, who was in the fifth grade, suddenly screamed out.

"Oh, I got it, he's goin' into the third grade!"

"That must be it," thought the little children.

Ichiro just stood there puzzled, with his head cocked to one side, as the weird new boy sat in his seat all prim and proper, staring back at them.

A strong gust of wind howled through the classroom and its glass doors rattled loudly, all the grasses and weeds and chestnut trees turned strangely pale, swaying back and forth, and the boy in the classroom started fidgeting in his seat with a big grin on his lips.

"Oh, I got it. He's Matasaburo, the boy of the winds!" shrieked Kasuke.

They all seemed to be agreeing with this, when Goro yelled out from behind.

"Ow! That hurts!" They all looked back. Kosuke had stepped on Goro's toes, and Goro blew his stack and was clobbering him. This sent Kosuke into a rage.

startled　驚いて、びっくりして

primly　「ちゃんと」、取りすまして

demeanor　「ぜんたいその形」、外見、振る舞い

baggy　「だぶだぶの」

googly eyes　（目が）「まん円」

jet black　「まっくろ」

stumped　「困って」、（言葉に）つまって

jabbered away　「がやがや」、ぺちゃくちゃしゃべり続ける

gust of wind　突風

grasses and weeds　「萱」

blew his stack　（カンカンに）「怒って」、激怒して

clobbering　「なぐりつけ」、打ちのめして

「早ぐ出はって来　出はって来」一郎が言いました。けれどもそのこどもはきょろきょろ室の中やみんなの方を見るばかりでやっぱりちゃんとひざに手をおいて腰掛に座っていました。

ぜんたいその形からが実におかしいのでした。変てこな鼠いろのだぶだぶの上着を着て白い半ずぼんをはいてそれに赤い革の半靴をはいていたのです。それに顔と言ったらまるで熟した苹果のよう、殊に眼はまん円でまっくろなのでした。一向語が通じないようなので一郎も全く困ってしまいました。

「あいつは外国人だな」「学校さ入るのだな。」みんなはがやがやがやがや言いました。ところが五年生の嘉助がいきなり

「ああ、三年生さ入るのだ。」と叫びましたので「ああそうだ。」と小さいこどもらは思いましたが一郎はだまってくびをまげました。

変なこどもはやはりきょろきょろこっちを見るだけきちんと腰掛けています。

そのとき風がどうと吹いて来て教室のガラス戸はみんながたがた鳴り、学校のうしろの山の萱や栗の木はみんな変に青じろくなってゆれ、教室のなかのこどもは何だかにやっとわらってすこしうごいたようでした。すると嘉助がすぐ叫びました。

「ああわかったあいつは風の又三郎だぞ。」

そうだっとみんなもおもったとき俄かにうしろの方で五郎が

「わあ、痛いじゃあ。」と叫びました。みんなそっちへ振り向きますと五郎が耕助に足のゆびをふまれてまるで怒って耕助をなぐりつけていたのです。すると耕助も怒って

"Ow!" shouted Kosuke, slugging Goro. "It was you who started punching me!"

Goro was bawling and his face was streaming with tears. He was doing his best to grapple with Kosuke. Ichiro wedged between them, and Kasuke took hold of Kosuke.

"Stop fighting," said Ichiro, looking through the window. "The teacher's already in his office."

But a cloud suddenly came over Ichiro's face. The strange boy who had been in the classroom but a moment ago had vanished into thin air. They all felt as if a pony they had just got to know had escaped to an unseen place or a little titmouse that they caught had flown away right between their fingers.

The wind was still howling raucously, rattling the glass doors, and pale waves rippled the grasses and weeds on the mountain behind the school.

"It's your fault for fighting and sending Matasaburo away!" said Kasuke, fuming.

Everyone agreed with this. Goro too felt it was all his fault. He forgot all about his pain and just stood there shrugging his shoulders.

"So that guy was Matasaburo, you mean?"

"Yeah, 'cause it's two hundred and ten days after the first day of spring."

"Yeah, an' he wore shoes."

"Yeah, an' he wore Western clothes."

"But he was a real weirdo with that red hair."

"Wait. He put stones on the desk!" said a second-grade pupil.

Sure enough, a bunch of small dirty stones had been left on the desk. "Yeah. Wait! He's smashed some of the glass in the doors!"

slugging　殴る、強打す
る

grapple with...　〜に
取り組む、〜に立ち向かう

wedged　「間へはいっ
て」、割り込ませて、押し
込んで

vanished into thin air
「影もかたちもない」、跡形
もなく消えた

titmouse　「山雀」

raucously　騒々しく、
耳障りに

fuming　「怒って」、頭か
ら湯気を立てて

shrugging his
shoulders　「肩をすぼめ
て」

weirdo　「おかしやづ」、
変なやつ

smashed　「ぶっかし
た」、ぶっ壊した、打ち砕
いた

「わあ、われ悪くてでひと撲いだなあ。」と言ってまた
五郎をなぐろうとしました。五郎はまるで顔中涙だらけ
にして耕助に組み付こうとしました。そこで一郎が間へ
はいって嘉助が耕助を押えてしまいました。

「わあい、喧嘩するなったら、先生ぁちゃんと職員室に
来てらぞ。」と一郎が言いながらまた教室の方を見まし
たら一郎は俄かにまるでぽかんとしてしまいました。たっ
たいままで教室にいたあの変な子が影もかたちもないの
です。みんなもまるでせっかく友達になった子うまが遠
くへやられたよう、せっかく捕った山雀に遁げられたよ
うに思いました。

　風がまたどうと吹いて来て窓ガラスをがたがた言わせ
うしろの山の萱をだんだん上流の方へ青じろく波だてて
行きました。

「わあうなだ喧嘩したんだから又三郎居なぐなった
な。」嘉助が怒って言いました。みんなもほんとうにそう
思いました。五郎はじつに申し訳けないと思って足の痛
いのも忘れてしょんぼり肩をすぼめて立ったのです。

「やっぱりあいつは風の又三郎だったな。」

「二百十日で来たのだな。」

「靴はいでだたぞ。」

「服も着でだたぞ。」

「髪赤くておかしやづだったな。」

「ありゃありゃ、又三郎おれの机の上さ石かげ乗せでっ
たぞ。」二年生の子が言いました。見るとその子の机の上
には汚ない石かけが乗っていたのです。

「そうだ。ありゃ。あそごのガラスもぶっかしたぞ。」

"Naw. That's from when Kaichi threw a rock at it before the summer break."

"Hell no! I didn't!" cried Kaichi.

By coincidence, that's just when the teacher came out the front door of the school into the yard. He held a shiny whistle in his right hand, getting ready to blow it to get the pupils to line up, and right behind him was none other than that red-haired boy, putting on airs, as if he was the loyal follower of some great spiritual leader, strolling all puffed up with a white cap on his head.

None of the children let out so much as a peep.

"Good morning, teacher," said Ichiro after a pause.

"Good morning, boys and girls," said the teacher, blowing hard on the whistle. "You all seem in high spirits today. All right then, let's line up." The whistle's whistle echoed off the mountains on the far side of the ravine right back to them as they lined up by grade, just as they did before the summer break. One pupil in the sixth grade. Seven in the fifth. Six in the fourth. Twelve in the third. Eight in the second and four in the first grade following suit, lining up like the others.

The weird little new boy stood all the while behind the teacher, staring at the other pupils with the sides of his tongue between his teeth, as if highly amused by the spectacle.

"All right, Takada," said the teacher, taking the boy to the fourth-grade row and, after comparing his height with Kasuke's, pointing to the space between him and Kiyo behind him, "line up here."

All the other pupils turned their gaze on the teacher, who was returning to the front.

"Now, fall in!" commanded the teacher.

「そだないでぁ。あいづぁ休み前に嘉一石ぶっつけだのだな。」

「わあい。そだないでぁ。」

と言っていたときこれはまた何という訳でしょう。先生が玄関から出て来たのです。先生はぴかぴか光る呼子を右手にもってもう集れの支度をしているのでしたが、そのすぐうしろから、さっきの赤い髪の子が、まるで権現さまの尾っぱ持ちのようにすまし込んで白いシャッポをかぶって先生についてすぱすぱとあるいて来たのです。

みんなはしいんとなってしまいました。やっと一郎が「先生お早うございます。」と言いましたのでみんなもついて「先生お早うございます」と言っただけでした。

「みなさん。お早う。どなたも元気ですね。では並んで。」先生は呼子をビルルと吹きました。それはすぐ谷の向うの山へひびいてまたピルルルと低く戻ってきました。

すっかりやすみの前の通りだとみんなが思いながら六年生は一人、五年生は七人、四年生は六人、三年生は十二人、組ごとに一列に縦にならびました。

二年は八人一年生は四人前へならえをしてならんだのです。するとその間あのおかしな子は何かおかしいのかおもしろいのか奥歯で横っちょに舌を嚙むようにしてじろじろみんなを見ながら先生のうしろに立っていたのです。すると先生は、高田さんこっちへおはいりなさいと言いながら四年生の列のところへ連れて行って丈を嘉助とくらべてから嘉助とそのうしろのきよの間へ立たせました。みんなはふりかえってじっとそれを見ていました。先生はまた玄関の前に戻って

前へならえと号令をかけました。

Naw 「そだないでぁ」、そうじゃない

By coincidence 偶然にも

whistle 「呼子」

putting on airs 「すまし込んで」、気取って、もったいぶって

loyal follower of some great spiritual leader 「権現さまの尾っぱ持ち」、偉いお坊さんの従者

strolling （ぶらぶら）「あるいて」

all puffed up 胸をいっぱいにして

in high spirits 「元気で」、意気揚々として

spectacle 光景、壮観

fall in 「前へならえ」

Everyone immediately fell into straight lines, but they were all so curious about what the weird new boy would do that they half turned around or tried to glimpse him out of the corner of their eye. But the new boy seemed to know exactly what to do and put out his hands to stand precisely at arms' length from Kasuke. As for Kasuke, he was all jerks and fidgets, as if his back was itchy or he was about to be tickled.

"Eyes to the front!" commanded the teacher again. "Now, forward from the first grade on!"

The first-grade pupils started to march forward, followed by the second and third grades, passing before all the others and entering the school from the right where the shoe cupboard was located. When the fourth-grade pupils were walking, the new boy, looking exceedingly pleased with himself, followed Kasuke. The pupils in front of him turned around to steal a look at him, while the ones behind couldn't stop staring at him.

Before long everyone's wooden clogs had been placed in the cupboard and they were sitting at their desk according to class, just as they had lined up outside. The new boy, looking all puffed up with himself like before, was sitting behind Kasuke. But that's when all hell broke loose in the classroom.

"Hey, this isn't my desk!"

"Hey, someone's put rocks on my desk!"

"Hey, Kikko, did'ya bring your report card? I forgot to bring mine."

"Listen, gimme your pencil, lend it to me, will ya?"

"Keep your mitts off my pencil!"

When the teacher walked in they all stood up noisily.

"Bow to the teacher!" said Ichiro from the very back.

みんなはもう一ぺん前へならえをしてすっかり列をつくりましたがじつはあの変な子がどういう風にしているのか見たくてかわるがわるそっちをふりむいたり横眼でにらんだりしたのでした。するとその子はちゃんと前へならえでもなんでも知ってるらしく平気で両腕を前へ出して指さきを嘉助のせなかへやっと届くくらいにしていたものですから嘉助は何だかせなかがかゆいかくすぐったいかという風にもじもじしていました。

「直れ」先生がまた号令をかけました。

「一年から順に前へおい。」

そこで一年生はあるき出しまもなく二年も三年もあるき出してみんなの前をぐるっと通って右手の下駄箱（げたばこ）のある入口に入って行きました。四年生があるき出すとさっきの子も嘉助のあとへついて大威張りであるいて行きました。前へ行った子もときどきふりかえって見、あとの者もじっと見ていたのです。

まもなくみんなははきものを下駄箱に入れて教室へ入って、ちょうど外へならんだときのように組ごとに一列に机に座りました。さっきの子もすまし込んで嘉助のうしろに座りました。ところがもう大さわぎです。

「わあ、おらの机代ってるぞ。」

「わあ、おらの机さ石かけ入ってるぞ。」

「キッコ、キッコ、うな通信簿持って来たが。おら忘れで来たじゃあ。」

「わあい、さの、木ペン借せ、木ペン借せったら。」

「わぁがない。ひとの雑記帳とってって。」

そのとき先生が入って来ましたのでみんなもさわぎながらとにかく立ちあがり一郎がいちばんうしろで「礼」と言いました。

jerks and fidgets 「もじもじして」(jerk: ガタガタと動く、fidget: そわそわする)

eyes to the front 「直れ」、かしらなか。軍の命令語

wooden clogs 「はきもの」、下駄

all hell broke loose 「大さわぎ」(になる)、大混乱が生じる

report card 「通信簿」、通知表

Keep your mitts off my pencil 「わぁがない。ひとの雑記帳とってって」、おれの鉛筆に触るな

The pupils stopped jabbering while they bowed but started blabbing to each other once standing straight again.

"Quiet, boys and girls!" said the teacher. "That's enough chattering!"

"Shhh!" said Ichiro to the loudest of them. "Etsuji, shut up. That means you too, Kasuke, and Kikko too."

This hushed them up.

"Boys and girls, I'm sure that you enjoyed your long summer vacation," said the teacher. "You all went swimming first thing in the morning and shouted in the woods louder than the hawks and helped the older boys with their mowing up at the fields. But today marks the end of your vacation and the beginning of the fall term. It has always been the case that the fall term has been thought of as the best one for concentrating on your studies. So, let's all buckle down and really study hard from now on. And, you've got a new classmate since the summer break. It's Takada who's sitting right there. His father's company has sent him to work up at the front of the field on the mountain. Until now Takada has been in school in Hokkaido, but from today he'll be your classmate, so I want you to ask him to study with you and to pick chestnuts and go fishing with him. Is that clear to everyone? If it is, please raise your hand."

All the pupils raised their hand right away. The new boy, Takada, raised his hand right up into the air too, bringing a faint smile to the teacher's lips.

"I see you all agree," he said. "We'll leave it at that."

They all lowered their hand as fast as a flame goes out.

みんなはおじぎをする間はちょっとしんとなりましたがそれからまたがやがやがやがや言いました。

　「しずかに、みなさん。しずかにするのです。」先生が言いました。

　「叱っ、悦治、やがましったら、嘉助ぇ、喜っこう。わあい。」と一郎が一番うしろからあまりさわぐものを一人ずつ叱りました。

　みんなはしんとなりました。先生が言いました。

　「みなさん長い夏のお休みは面白かったですね。みなさんは朝から水泳ぎもできたし林の中で鷹にも負けないくらい高く叫んだりまた兄さんの草刈りについて上の野原へ行ったりしたでしょう。けれどももう昨日で休みは終りました。これからは第二学期で秋です。むかしから秋は一番からだこころもひきしまって勉強のできる時だといってあるのです。ですから、みなさんも今日からまたいっしょにしっかり勉強しましょう。それからこのお休みの間にみなさんのお友達が一人ふえました。それはそこに居る高田さんです。その方のお父さんはこんど会社のご用で上の野原の入り口へおいでになっていられるのです。高田さんはいままでは北海道の学校に居られたのですが今日からみなさんのお友達になるのですから、みなさんは学校で勉強のときも、また栗拾いや魚とりに行くときも高田さんをさそうようにしなければなりません。わかりましたか。わかった人は手をあげてごらんなさい。」

　すぐみんなは手をあげました。その高田とよばれた子も勢よく手をあげましたので、ちょっと先生はわらいましたがすぐ、

　「わかりましたね、ではよし。」と言いましたのでみんなは火の消えたように一ぺんに手をおろしました。

blabbing　「がやがや」（言う）、べらべらしゃべる

mowing　「草刈り」

buckle down　身を引き締める、精を出す

風の又三郎　27

"Teacher?" said Kasuke, raising his hand again.

"What is it?" he said, pointing to him.

"What's Takada's given name?"

"It's Saburo."

"Wow, I guessed it! He really is Matasaburo!"

Kasuke clapped his hands and was all but dancing at his desk. This made the older children burst into laughter, but the littler ones just stared at Saburo in silence, as if he was somehow scary.

"Now, boys and girls," said the teacher, "you were all supposed to bring your report card signed by your parents and your homework. Please place them on your desk and I'll come around and pick them up."

All of them hurriedly opened their school bags or undid the knots on their furoshiki cloths and put their report card and homework on their desk. The teacher went around collecting them, starting with the first-grade pupils. But, without warning, they were given a jolt. A man who wasn't there before was seen at the back of the class. He was just standing there smiling faintly while gazing over the pupils. He was dressed in a loose-fitting white linen suit, had a glossy black bandana around his neck instead of a necktie, and in his hand he held a white fan that he was lightly fanning his face with. The sight of him quietened down all the pupils and they just stood where they were like statues. The teacher acted as if the man was not there at all. He just went around from desk to desk picking up the report cards. When he came to Saburo's desk he saw that there was neither report card nor homework on it. The only thing on Saburo's desk were his two clenched fists. But the teacher walked right on by without speaking and, after finishing his round, straightened out all the papers in his hands and returned to the front.

ところが嘉助がすぐ「先生。」といってまた手をあげました。

「はい、」先生は嘉助を指さしました。

「高田さん名は何て言うべな。」

「高田三郎さんです。」

「わあ、うまい、そりゃ、やっぱり又三郎だな。」嘉助はまるで手を叩いて机の中で踊るようにしましたので、大きな方の子どもらはどっと笑いましたが三年生から下の子どもらは何か怖いという風にしいんとして三郎の方を見ていたのです。先生はまた言いました。

「今日はみなさんは通信簿と宿題をもってくるのでしたね。持って来た人は机の上へ出してください。私がいま集めに行きますから。」

みんなはばたばた鞄をあけたり風呂敷をといたりして通信簿と宿題帖を机の上に出しました。

そして先生が一年生の方から順にそれを集めはじめました。そのときみんなはぎょっとしました。という訳はみんなのうしろのところにいつか一人の大人が立っていたのです。その人は白いだぶだぶの麻服を着て黒いてかてかした半巾をネクタイの代りに首に巻いて手には白い扇をもって軽くじぶんの顔を扇ぎながら少し笑ってみんなを見おろしていたのです。さあみんなはだんだんしいんとなってまるで堅くなってしまいました。ところが先生は別にその人を気にかける風もなく順々に通信簿を集めて三郎の席まで行きますと三郎は通信簿も宿題帖もない代りに両手をにぎりこぶしにして二つ机の上にのせていたのです。先生はだまってそこを通りすぎ、みんなのを集めてしまうとそれを両手でそろえながらまた教壇に戻りました。

given a jolt 「ぎょっとし」、ショックを与えられ

gazing over... 「〜を見おろして」、〜をじっと眺めて

linen suit 「麻服」

clenched fists 「にぎりこぶし」

"So, I'll be giving you back your corrected homework this Saturday, so those who didn't bring it today please bring it without fail tomorrow. And I'm talking about Etsuji, Koji and Ryosaku. That will be all for today. Please come prepared from tomorrow as you always have. Fifth and sixth grade, please stay behind and assist with cleaning the classroom. Class dismissed."

"Attention!" said Ichiro, as they all stood up together. Even the man in back lowered his fan and stood straight.

"Bow!"

They all bowed, including the teacher and the man in back, who did so with a nod. The littler children dashed out of the room. Those in the fourth grade were fidgeting in their seats. Saburo made his way to the man in the baggy white suit in the back, and they were joined by the teacher.

"All I can say is thank you very much," said the man, politely bowing to the teacher.

"I'm sure that Saburo will become good friends with everyone right away," said the teacher, returning the bow.

"I'm grateful for everything you are doing for him," said the man, bowing again. "We'll be off now."

He signaled to Saburo that they should go, walked over to the entrance and out, waiting by the door for Saburo to follow. Saburo, wide-eyed and aware that everyone was looking at him, took himself to the side entrance and left, then followed the man across the yard. He took one more look back from the edge of the yard, as if glaring at the school and the children, then rushed to catch up with the man in the white suit on the path that led downriver.

「では宿題帖はこの次の土曜日に直して渡しますから、今日持って来なかった人は、あしたきっと忘れないで持って来てください。それは悦治さんとコージさんとリョウサクさんとですね。では今日はここまでです。あしたからちゃんといつもの通りの支度をしてお出でなさい。それから五年生と六年生の人は、先生といっしょに教室のお掃除をしましょう。ではここまで。」

一郎が気を付けと言いみんなは一ぺんに立ちました。うしろの大人も扇を下にさげて立ちました。

「礼。」先生もみんなも礼をしました。うしろの大人も軽く頭を下げました。それからずうっと下の組の子どもらは一目散に教室を飛び出しましたが四年生の子どもらはまだもじもじしていました。

すると三郎はさっきのだぶだぶの白い服の人のところへ行きました。先生も教壇を下りてその人のところへ行きました。

「いやどうもご苦労さまでございます。」その大人はていねいに先生に礼をしました。

「じきみんなとお友達になりますから、」先生も礼を返しながら言いました。

「何分どうかよろしくおねがいいたします。それでは。」その人はまたていねいに礼をして眼で三郎に合図すると自分は玄関の方へまわって外へ出て待っていますと三郎はみんなの見ている中を眼をりんとはってだまって昇降口から出て行って追いつき二人は運動場を通って川下の方へ歩いて行きました。

運動場を出るときその子はこっちをふりむいてじっと学校やみんなの方をにらむようにするとまたすたすた白服の大人について歩いて行きました。

Class dismissed （授業は）「ここまで」

We'll be off now 「それでは」、もう行きます

"Sir, is that man Saburo's dad?" asked Ichiro with a broom in his hand.

"That's right, he is."

"What does he do here?"

"He's here to get things ready to dig out molybdenum, which is a kind of metal, that's in the ground around the front of the field up the mountain."

"Whereabouts up there?"

"I'm not sure myself, but you know the old horse path that everyone uses? I think it's a bit downriver from that."

"What does that molybdenum stuff do?"

"Well, it's used in steel alloys and it can apparently be a medicine as well."

"Does that mean Matasaburo's diggin' it up too?" asked Kasuke.

"Don't call him Matasaburo. His name's Takada Saburo," said Sataro.

"No, it's Matasaburo. Matasaburo!" insisted Kasuke, his face now red as a beet.

"If you're just standin' around like that, give us a hand here," said Ichiro.

"No way. It's the kids in the fifth and sixth grade whose turn it is today!"

At that, Kasuke flew out of the classroom.

A wind rose again, the window glass rattled and the black surface of the water in a bucket with a wiping cloth in it rippled and swished.

「先生、あの人は高田さんのお父さんですか。」一郎が<ruby>箒<rt>ほうき</rt></ruby>をもちながら先生にききました。

「そうです。」

「なんの用で来たべ。」

「上の野原の入口にモリブデンという鉱石ができるので、それをだんだん掘るようにする<ruby>為<rt>ため</rt></ruby>だそうです。」

「どこらあだりだべな。」

「私もまだよくわかりませんが、いつもみなさんが馬をつれて行くみちから少し川下へ寄った方なようです。」

「モリブデン何にするべな。」

「それは鉄とまぜたり、薬をつくったりするのだそうです。」

「そだら又三郎も掘るべが。」<ruby>嘉助<rt>かすけ</rt></ruby>が言いました。

「又三郎だない。高田三郎だぢゃ。」佐太郎が言いました。

「又三郎だ又三郎だ。」嘉助が顔をまっ赤にしてがん張りました。

「嘉助、うなも残ってらば掃除してすけろ。」一郎が言いました。

「わぁい。やんたじゃ。きょう五年生ど六年生だな。」

嘉助は大急ぎで教室をはねだして<ruby>遁<rt>に</rt></ruby>げてしまいました。

風がまた吹いて来て窓ガラスはまたがたがた鳴り<ruby>雑巾<rt>ぞうきん</rt></ruby>を入れたバケツにも小さな黒い波をたてました。

molybdenum 「モリブデン」。クロミウムおよびタングステンと性質が似た、多価の金属元素。鋼鉄の強度と硬度を上げるのに用いられる

steel alloys 合金

red as a beet 「まっ赤」な

2 September

Ichiro was dying to get to school the next day to see if that weird new boy was there doing his schoolwork, and he went over to Kasuke's really early so they could go together. But Kasuke had the same thought and, having wolfed down his breakfast, was already standing in front of Ichiro's house with a furoshiki full of books. They couldn't stop talking about the new boy on their way to school. Several of the little children were playing hide-the-stick in the school yard. The new boy apparently hadn't been through there yet. Maybe, they thought, he was already in the classroom like the day before, but when they peeked into the room there wasn't a soul there. All they saw was hazy white stripes left on the blackboard by the wiping cloth from the day before.

"The kid from yesterday hasn't come yet," said Ichiro.

"Yeah," said Kasuke, looking through the window all around the room.

Ichiro went under the horizontal bar and, pulling himself up by huffs and puffs until he finally made it up, managed to sit on the side bar by gripping it with both hands together, determined to stay right there so that he could keep a close watch on the path that Matasaburo left school by the day before. The river glistened as it flowed, and the weeds and reeds rose in white waves as the wind blew over the mountains.

Kasuke stood by the poles that propped up the bar. He also had his eyes peeled on the path that Matasaburo had taken. It didn't take long before Matasaburo was running up the path, clutching his gray school bag in his right hand.

九月二日

　次の日一郎はあのおかしな子供が今日からほんとうに学校へ来て本を読んだりするかどうか早く見たいような気がしていつもより早く嘉助をさそいました。ところが嘉助の方は一郎よりもっとそう考えていたと見えてとうにごはんもたべふろしきに包んだ本ももって家の前へ出て一郎を待っていたのでした。二人は途中もいろいろその子のことを談しながら学校へ来ました。すると運動場には小さな子供らがもう七八人集まっていて棒かくしをしていましたがその子はまだ来ていませんでした。また昨日のように教室の中に居るのかと思って中をのぞいて見ましたが教室の中はしいんとして誰も居ず黒板の上には昨日掃除のとき雑巾で拭いた痕が乾いてぼんやり白い縞になっていました。

　「昨日のやつまだ来てないな。」一郎が言いました。

　「うん。」嘉助も言ってそこらを見まわしました。

　一郎はそこで鉄棒の下へ行ってじゃみ上りというやり方で無理やりに鉄棒の上にのぼり両腕をだんだん寄せて右の腕木に行くとそこへ腰掛けて昨日又三郎の行った方をじっと見おろして待っていました。谷川はそっちの方へきらきら光ってながれて行きその下の山の上の方では風も吹いているらしくときどき萱が白く波立っていました。嘉助もやっぱりその柱の下でじっとそっちを見て待っていました。ところが二人はそんなに永く待つこともありませんでした。それは突然又三郎がその下手のみちから灰いろの鞄を右手にかかえて走るようにして出て来たのです。

wolfed down　急いで食べた、むさぼり食った

hide-the-stick　「棒かくし」。決められた範囲に1人が棒を隠し、残りのものがそれを探す遊び

soul　（否定文で）人っ子一人（いない）

horizontal bar　「鉄棒」

huffs and puffs　息を切らす、息を弾ませる

reeds　萱

"He's here!" blurted out Ichiro to Kasuke below him.

Matasaburo was already making his way around the embankment and through the school gate.

"Morning," he called out in a clear voice. They all looked his way, but no one said a thing in return.

They had all been taught from the very beginning that you had to say "Good morning" to each other every day. Even so, they were really flustered by Matasaburo saying it and in such a nice high-spirited way to boot, so they somehow managed to mumble some garbled words, but it was definitely nothing resembling a "Good morning."

Matasaburo was totally unfazed by this. He took a couple of steps forward, stopped and gazed all around the yard with those jet-black eyes of his. It seemed like he was looking for someone to play with. The others stared at him but somehow continued to busy themselves with things like playing hide-the-stick at the same time. Not one of them went up to Matasaburo. He just stood there as if frozen to the spot and out of place, gazing around the yard.

He then started taking big strides across the yard, as if measuring how far it exactly was from the gate to the front door of the school. Ichiro abruptly jumped down from the bar and stood beside Kasuke. They both held their breath and stared at Matasaburo. When Matasaburo made it to the front door he turned toward them and cocked his head to the side, like you do when you're doing mental arithmetic. None of the children could take their eyes off him. Finally, he put his hands together behind his back as if troubled by something and started to walk past the teacher's office toward the embankment on the other side.

school gate 「正門」

flustered 「臆して」、動揺して、うろたえて

mumble some garbled words 「もにゃもにゃっと言って」（garbled: 不明瞭な、しどろもどろの）

unfazed 「苦にする風もなく」、動じずに、臆せずに

stood there as if frozen 「そこにつっ立っていました」

out of place 「工合が悪いように」、場違いのように

big strides 「大股」

mental arithmetic 「諳算」

「来たぞ」と一郎が思わず下に居る嘉助へ叫ぼうとしていますと早くも又三郎はどてをぐるっとまわってどんどん正門を入って来ると

「お早う。」とはっきり言いました。みんなはいっしょにそっちをふり向きましたが一人も返事をしたものがありませんでした。それはみんなは先生にはいつでも「お早うございます」というように習っていたのでしたがお互に「お早う」なんて言ったことがなかったのに又三郎にそう言われても一郎や嘉助はあんまりにわかでまた勢がいいのでとうとう臆<ruby>臆<rt>おく</rt></ruby>してしまって一郎も嘉助も口の中でお早うというかわりにもにゃもにゃっと言ってしまったのでした。ところが又三郎の方はべつだんそれを苦にする風もなく二三歩また前へ進むとじっと立ってそのまっ黒な眼でぐるっと運動場じゅうを見まわしました。そしてしばらく誰か遊ぶ相手がないかさがしているようでした。けれどもみんなきょろきょろ又三郎の方は見ていてももじもじしてやはり忙しそうに棒かくしをしたり又三郎の方へ行くものがありませんでした。又三郎はちょっと工合<ruby>工<rt>ぐ</rt>合<rt>あい</rt></ruby>が悪いようにそこにつっ立っていましたがまた運動場をもう一度見まわしました。それからぜんたいこの運動場は何間あるかというように正門から玄関まで大股<ruby>大股<rt>おおまた</rt></ruby>に歩数を数えながら歩きはじめました。一郎は急いで鉄棒をはねおりて嘉助とならんで息をこらしてそれを見ていました。

そのうち又三郎は向うの玄関の前まで行ってしまうとこっちへ向いてしばらく諳算<ruby>諳算<rt>あんざん</rt></ruby>をするように少し首をまげて立っていました。

みんなはやはりきろきろそっちを見ています。又三郎は少し困ったように両手をうしろへ組むと向う側の土手の方へ職員室の前を通って歩きだしました。

Just at that moment a strong gust of wind passed through the yard, sending whirlwinds of dust into the air, and the grasses on the embankment rustled in waves. When the gust struck the front door of the school, little whorls of wind wound around, climbing higher than the roof in what looked like yellow dust coming out of jars turned upside down.

"That's him doin' it!" screamed Kasuke. "It's all because of him, Matasaburo! Whenever he does something, the wind blows."

"Yeah," said Ichiro, though he really wasn't sure and looked back at Saburo again.

As for Matasaburo, he was simply walking at a brisk pace toward the embankment as if nothing at all had happened.

"Good morning," said all the little children to the teacher, who was coming out of the school with his whistle in hand.

"Good morning," said the teacher, looking around the yard. "Well, line up, please," he added, blowing his whistle.

All the children lined up straight, just as they had done the day before, and Matasaburo, too, was standing where he was supposed to be. The teacher gave out his instructions, squinting from the light of the sun that was shining right into his eyes, and after that all the children went to the classroom through the side entrance. "So, today we begin our studies in earnest," he said, after the standing and bowing formalities were over. "You've all brought everything you need, I trust. Now, first grade and second grade, take out your penmanship textbooks and your inkstones, also third and fourth grade, your arithmetic and general exercise books and pencils, fifth and sixth grade, your Japanese textbooks."

その時風がざあっと吹いて来て土手の草はざわざわ波になり運動場のまん中でさあっと塵があがりそれが玄関の前まで行くときりきりとまわって小さなつむじ風になって黄いろな塵は瓶をさかさまにしたような形になって屋根より高くのぼりました。すると嘉助が突然高く言いました。

「そうだ。やっぱりあいづ又三郎だぞ。あいつ何かするときっと風吹いてくるぞ。」

「うん。」一郎はどうだかわからないと思いながらもだまってそっちを見ていました。又三郎はそんなことにはかまわず土手の方へやはりすたすたと歩いて行きます。

そのとき先生がいつものように呼子をもって玄関を出て来たのです。

「お早うございます。」小さな子どもらははせ集りました。

「お早う。」先生はちらっと運動場中を見まわしてから「ではならんで。」と言いながらプルルッと笛を吹きました。

みんなは集ってきて昨日のとおりきちんとならびました。又三郎も昨日言われた所へちゃんと立っています。先生はお日さまがまっ正面なのですこしまぶしそうにしながら号令をだんだんかけてとうとうみんなは昇降口から教室へ入りました。そして礼がすむと先生は

「ではみなさん今日から勉強をはじめましょう。みなさんはちゃんとお道具をもってきましたね。では一年生と二年生の人はお習字のお手本と硯と紙を出して、三年生と四年生の人は算術帳と雑記帳と鉛筆を出して五年生と六年生の人は国語の本を出してください。」

---

sending whirlwinds of dust into the air 塵が空にくるくる舞い上がり

little whorls of wind 「小さなつむじ風」

at a brisk pace 「すたすた」

squinting （まぶしい光などに）目を細めて

in earnest 真剣に、本格的に

standing and bowing formalities 「礼」

penmanship 「お習字」

inkstones 「硯」

arithmetic 「算術」

general exercise books 「雑記帳」

風の又三郎 39

But the class broke into an unbelievable commotion. Sataro, who was in the fourth grade and whose desk was right next to Matasaburo's, stuck his hand over to third-grade Kayo's desk and snatched her pencil off it, and she was his little sister!

"Sataro, gimme back my pencil!" she said, reaching out to get it.

"No, it's mine!" he said, slipping the pencil into an inside pocket and, putting both hands in his sleeves like the Chinese do when they bow to each other, leaning forward to lay his chest over his desk.

"You lost your pencil in the back shed the day before yesterday," she said, standing up and trying as hard as she could to get it back. "Give it back!"

But Sataro was sprawling over his desk like a fossilized crab, and all Kayo could do was stand there with a big twisted grimace on her face as if she was about to bawl her eyes out.

Matasaburo, who had been staring at his Japanese textbook and wondering what to do, noticed that Kayo was all teary and, reaching over to Sataro's desk with his right hand, put his half-worn-down pencil on it. This suddenly brightened Sataro's mood and he bolted up.

"You givin' me this?" he asked.

"Uh-huh," said Matasaburo, after a moment's fluster.

Sataro smiled, reached into his inside pocket, took out the pencil and placed it in Kayo's little pink palm.

The teacher was putting water on a first-grade pupil's inkstone some desks away so he didn't see what happened, and neither did Kasuke, who was sitting in front of Matasaburo, but Ichiro had seen it all from his seat in the very back of the room and was overcome with a strange feeling and at a total loss for words.

commotion 「大さわ
ぎ」、騒動

back shed 「小屋」

sprawling over his
desk 机の上に手を広げ
て、寝そべり

fossilized crab 「蟹の
化石」

with a big twisted
grimace 「口を大きくま
げて」(grimace: しかめっ
面)

bawl her eyes out
「泣きだし」、大声で泣き、
泣き叫び

half-worn-down 「半
分ばかりになった」(wear
down: すり減る、磨滅す
る)

bolted up 「むっくり起
き上り」、飛び起き

at a total loss for
words 「何と言ったらい
いかわからない」

　さあするとあっちでもこっちでも大さわぎがはじま
りました。中にも又三郎のすぐ横の四年生の机の佐太郎
がいきなり手をのばして三年生のかよの鉛筆をひらりと
とってしまったのです。かよは佐太郎の妹でした。する
とかよは
　「うわあ兄な木ペン取ってわかんないな。」と言いなが
ら取り返そうとしますと佐太郎が
　「わあこいつおれのだなあ。」と言いながら鉛筆をふと
ころの中へ入れてあとは支那人がおじぎするときのよう
に両手を袖へ入れて机へぴったり胸をくっつけました。
するとかよは立って来て、
　「兄な、兄なの木ペンは一昨日小屋で無くしてしまったけ
なあ。よこせったら。」と言いながら一生けん命とり返そ
うとしましたがどうしてももう佐太郎は机にくっついた大
きな蟹の化石みたいになっているのでとうとうかよは立っ
たまま口を大きくまげて泣きだしそうになりました。する
と又三郎は国語の本をちゃんと机にのせて困ったようにし
てこれを見ていましたがかよがとうとうぼろぼろ涙をこぼ
したのを見るとだまって右手に持っていた半分ばかりに
なった鉛筆を佐太郎の眼の前の机に置きました。すると佐
太郎はにわかに元気になってむっくり起き上りました。そ
して「呉れる？」と又三郎にききました。又三郎はちょっ
とまごついたようでしたが覚悟したように「うん」と言い
ました。すると佐太郎はいきなりわらい出してふところの
鉛筆をかよの小さな赤い手に持たせました。
　先生は向うで一年生の子の硯に水をついでやったりし
ていましたし嘉助は又三郎の前ですから知りませんでした
が一郎はこれをいちばんうしろでちゃんと見ていました。
　そしてまるで何と言ったらいいかわからない変な気持
ちがして歯をきりきり言わせました。

"Now, I want the third-grade pupils to review subtraction that you did before the summer break," said the teacher, writing "25 minus 12" on the board. "I want you to solve this."

All of the third-grade pupils, including Kayo, stuck their face right into their exercise book.

"Fourth grade, this is for you," he said, writing "17 times 4" on the board.

All the fourth-grade pupils, including Sataro, Kizo and Kosuke, copied the problem in their exercise book.

"Now, fifth-grade pupils, read to yourself from your readers from where we left off last time. Make sure you write down any characters you don't know in your exercise book." The fifth-grade pupils started reading to themselves.

"You too, Ichiro. Look through your reader from where you left off and pick out the characters you don't know."

Having said that, the teacher stepped down from the board and went around the desks of the first- and second-grade pupils, checking their penmanship.

Matasaburo held his book properly in both hands on his desk and concentrated intently on reading from where he was supposed to. But he wasn't writing down any characters in his exercise book, and it was hard to say if it was because he knew all of them or because he had given his only pencil to Sataro.

The teacher returned to the board and wrote the right answers to the problems he had given the pupils in the third and fourth grade on it, before giving them new problems to solve. Then he wrote the characters that the fifth-grade pupils had copied into their exercise book on the board and, next to them, the readings and meanings of those characters.

「では三年生のひとはお休みの前にならった引き算をもう一ぺん習ってみましょう。これを勘定してごらんなさい。」先生は黒板に $\frac{25}{-12}$ と書きました。三年生のこどもらはみんな一生けん命にそれを雑記帖にうつしました。かよも頭を雑記帖へくっつけるようにして書いています。「四年生の人はこれを置いて」$\frac{17}{\times 4}$ と書きました。四年生は佐太郎をはじめ喜蔵も甲助もみんなそれをうつしました。

　「五年生の人は読本の〔一字空白〕頁（ページ）の〔一字不明〕課をひらいて声をたてないで読めるだけ読んでごらんなさい。わからない字は雑記帖へ拾って置くのです。」五年生もみんな言われたとおりしはじめました。

　「一郎さんは読本の〔一字空白〕頁をしらべてやはり知らない字を書き抜いてください。」

　それがすむと先生はまた教壇を下りて一年生と二年生の習字を一人一人見てあるきました。又三郎は両手で本をちゃんと机の上へもって言われたところを息もつかずじっと読んでいました。けれども雑記帖へは字を一つも書き抜いていませんでした。それはほんとうに知らない字が一つもないのかたった一本の鉛筆を佐太郎にやってしまったためかどっちともわかりませんでした。

　そのうち先生は教壇へ戻って三年生と四年生の算術の計算をして見せてまた新らしい問題を出すと今度は五年生の生徒の雑記帖へ書いた知らない字を黒板へ書いてそれをかなとわけをつけました。そして

board 「黒板」
concentrated intently
「息もつかずじっと」、熱心に、一心に

"All right, Kasuke," he said, pointing to a page in the textbook, "read from here."

Kasuke faltered over a few characters, but the teacher gave him a hand. Matasaburo just sat there taking it all in. The teacher, with book in hand, listened to Kasuke read, but stopped him after about ten lines.

"That will do," he said, starting to read aloud himself.

He read through that part and then told the pupils to pack their things in their bags.

"All right, we'll stop here now," he said from the board.

"Attention!" said Ichiro from the back.

They all bowed and filed outside. But now instead of forming rows they ran about in all directions and played.

During the second hour they practiced choir. The teacher brought out a mandolin and accompanied them in all five songs they had learned. Matasaburo knew the songs too and sang along at the top of his lungs. The time flew by in no time.

During the third hour the pupils in the third and fourth grade studied Japanese, while the fifth and sixth grade did math, with the teacher writing problems to solve on the blackboard. Ichiro wrote down his answers while stealing glances at Matasaburo. For his part, Matasaburo produced a little chunk of charcoal from out of nowhere and furiously began his calculations.

「では嘉助さんここを読んで」と言いました。嘉助は二三度ひっかかりながら先生に教えられて読みました。

又三郎もだまって聞いていました。先生も本をとってじっと聞いていましたが十行ばかり読むと

「そこまで」と言ってこんどは先生が読みました。

そうして一まわり済むと先生はだんだんみんなの道具をしまわせました。それから

「ではここまで」と言って教壇に立ちますと一郎がうしろで

「気をつけい」と言いました。そして礼がすむとみんな順に外へ出てこんどは外へならばずにみんな別れ別れになって遊びました。

二時間目は一年生から六年生までみんな唱歌でした。そして先生がマンドリンをもって出て来てみんなはいままでに唱ったのを先生のマンドリンについて五つもうたいました。

又三郎もみんな知っていてみんなどんどん歌いました。そしてこの時間は大へん早くたってしまいました。

三時間目になるとこんどは三年生と四年生が国語で五年生と六年生が数学でした。先生はまた黒板に問題を書いて五年生と六年生に計算させました。しばらくたって一郎が答えを書いてしまうと又三郎の方をちょっと見ました。すると又三郎はどこから出したか小さな消し炭で雑記帖の上へがりがりと大きく運算していたのです。

faltered 「ひっかかり」、行き詰まり、筆が渋り

taking it all in 「だまって聞いて」、すべてを把握しようとして

Attention 「気をつけ」

filed outside 「外へ出て」、出ていき

choir 「唱歌」

mandolin 「マンドリン」

at the top of his lungs 声を張りあげて、声を限りに

little chunk of charcoal 「小さな消し炭」

furiously 「がりがりと」、激しく、荒々しく

Sunday, 4 September

The next morning the sky was translucent and clear, and the river in the ravine murmured as it flowed along. Ichiro went around to Kasuke's and Sataro's and Etsuji's before they all proceeded to Saburo's house.

They crossed the river a bit downstream and all broke off a branch from the willow tree on the bank and made whips by peeling off the green bark as they would the skin of an apple and whirling them around in the air as they made their way in a flurry up the road to the field on the mountain. Before long they were out of breath.

"D'ya think Matasaburo's really waitin' for us by the spring?"

"Sure he is. Matasaburo wouldn't lie."

"It's so hot. I wish a wind would blow."

"There's a wind comin' from somewhere."

"Yeah, Matasaburo's bringin' it on!"

"Gee, the sun's gone all dim."

A gauze of cloud now covered the sky. The boys had made it quite a ways up the mountain. Everyone's house down in the valley looked minute and the shed roof at Ichiro's house was reflecting a white light. The road had turned into a forest and for some time was all soggy. They couldn't see far through the dark. But they were soon approaching the spring where Saburo had promised to meet them. That's when they heard him shout out to them.

"Hullo! Is that you guys?"

九月四日、日曜

　次の朝空はよく晴れて谷川はさらさら鳴りました。一郎は途中で嘉助と佐太郎と悦治をさそって一緒に三郎のうちの方へ行きました。学校の少し下流で谷川をわたって、それから岸で楊の枝をみんなで一本ずつ折って青い皮をくるくる剝いで鞭を拵えて手でひゅうひゅう振りながら上の野原への路をだんだんのぼって行きました。みんなは早くも登りながら息をはあはあしました。

　「又三郎ほんとにあそごの湧水まで来て待ぢでるべが。」

　「待ぢでるんだ。又三郎偽こがないもな。」

　「ああ暑う、風吹げばいいな。」

　「どごがらだが風吹いでるぞ。」

　「又三郎吹がせだらべも。」

　「何だがお日さんぼゃっとして来たな。」

　空に少しばかりの白い雲が出ました。そしてもう大分のぼっていました。谷のみんなの家がずうっと下に見え、一郎のうちの木小屋の屋根が白く光っています。

　道が林の中に入り、しばらく路はじめじめして、あたりは見えなくなりました。そして間もなくみんなは約束の湧水の近くに来ました。するとそこから

　「おうい。みんな来たかい。」と三郎の高く叫ぶ声がしました。

murmured　せせらいだ、ざわめいた（murmur: せせらぎ）

willow tree　「楊」

whips　「鞭」

green bark　「青い皮」

whirling... around　〜をぐるぐる回す

spring　「湧水」

dim　薄暗く、ほの暗く

gauze of cloud　「少しばかりの（白い）雲」

looked minute　とても小さく見えた

soggy　「じめじめ」、（地面などが水で）ぐちゃぐちゃ、ぬるぬる

At this they all hustled up the road toward him, and when they turned a corner, Matasaburo was there watching them with his thin lips clamped tightly shut. They finally made it to him but they were panting so hard they couldn't get a word out. Kasuke, for one, was really impatient to speak, but all he could do was look up at the sky and loudly expel a "Whew!"

"I've been expecting you for ages," cried Saburo with a laugh. "And, you know, they say it might rain today too."

"We all better beat it then. I just wanna have a drink from the spring first."

The four boys wiped the sweat from their brow, crouched down and, cupping their hands, drank the cold water that was bubbling out from the white boulder.

"I live right near here," said Matasaburo. "It's just above that valley over there. It'd be great if you all stopped in."

"Great. But first we gotta go to the field."

The four of them started on their way. The water in the spring creaked and rumbled, as if trying to tell them something, and all the trees around them roared and grumbled. They crossed through the thickets and groves, passing many places where the boulders had tumbled into stones and pebbles, until they finally got close to the gate at the field. They all turned around to view the road they had taken below the western sky. The fields and meadows that skirted the river spread out hazy blue in the distance beyond the countless hills piled one onto the other, and it all was bathed now in brilliant light, now in gloom.

"Wow, I can see the river!"

"It's like the cloth that hangs down on the rope from the bell at Kasuga Shrine," said Matasaburo.

"Like what?" asked Ichiro.

みんなはまるでせかせかと走ってのぼりました。向うの曲り角の処に又三郎が小さな唇をきっと結んだまま三人のかけ上って来るのを見ていました。三人はやっと三郎の前まで来ました。けれどもあんまり息がはあはあしてすぐには何も言えませんでした。嘉助などはあんまりもどかしいもんですから、空へ向いて

「ホッホウ。」と叫んで早く息を吐いてしまおうとしました。すると三郎は大きな声で笑いました。

「ずいぶん待ったぞ。それに今日は雨が降るかもしれないそうだよ。」

「そだら早ぐ行ぐべさ。おらまんつ水呑んでぐ。」

三人は汗をふいてしゃがんでまっ白な岩からごぼごぼ噴きだす冷たい水を何べんも掬ってのみました。

「ぼくのうちはここからすぐなんだ。ちょうどあの谷の上あたりなんだ。みんなで帰りに寄ろうねえ。」

「うん。まんつ野原さ行ぐべさ。」

みんながまたあるきはじめたとき湧水は何かを知らせるようにぐうっと鳴り、そこらの樹もなんだかざあっと鳴ったようでした。

四人は林の裾の藪の間を行ったり岩かけの小さく崩れる所を何べんも通ったりしてもう上の原の入口に近くなりました。

みんなはそこまで来ると来た方からまた西の方をながめました。光ったり陰ったり幾通りにも重なったたくさんの丘の向うに川に沿ったほんとうの野原がぼんやり碧くひろがっているのでした。

「ありゃ、あいづ川だぞ。」

「春日明神さんの帯のようだな。」又三郎が言いました。

「何のようだど。」一郎がききました。

---

hustled 「走って」、急いで駆ける

clamped tightly shut 「きっと結んだ」、しっかりと締めた

panting 「息がはあはあして」、息を切らして

expel 「吐いて」、吐き出して

beat it 「早ぐ行ぐ」、出ていく

crouched down 「しゃがんで」

boulder 「岩」、巨礫

tumbled 「崩れる」

pebble 小石、砂利

meadow 「野原」、草地

skirted 「沿った」

hazy 「ぼんやり」、かすんだ

bathed... in gloom 「陰ったり」、薄暗くなったり

cloth that hangs down on the rope from the bell at Kasuga Shrine 「春日明神さんの帯」。春日神社の礼拝所に梁から吊り下げられている銅製の鰐口を鳴らすための綱と一緒に垂らしている布

"Like the cloth that hangs down on the rope from the bell at Kasuga Shrine."

"You mean, you've seen the cloth that the gods got?"

"Yep. I saw it in Hokkaido."

They all had no idea at all what he was talking about and found themselves at a total loss for words.

There was a single huge chestnut tree in the neatly cut grass by the gate to the field, its trunk growing from roots rising out of a large burntblack hole; and hanging from its branches were shreds of old rope and tatters of straw sandals.

"There're people cuttin' the grass up there," said Ichiro, as he forged ahead on a path that ran through the mowed grass. "An' they got horses up there too."

"They can let the horses run free up here," said Saburo, who was right behind him. "Because there are no bears up here."

Tall oak trees lined the path up from there, and under the trees hemp bags were lying about and bundles of grass were scattered around.

Two horses with a load of grass bundles on their back sniffed and snorted when they caught sight of Ichiro.

"Hey, is my brother up there?" yelled Ichiro, wiping the sweat from his brow. "Tell him his little brother's here!"

"Yup!" shouted Ichiro's brother from a hollow beyond the horses. "I'm here! Stay there, I'll be there in two shakes of a lamb's tail!"

The sun came blindingly out and Ichiro's older brother emerged from the tall grass, beaming.

「春日明神さんの帯のようだ。」

「うな神さんの帯見だごとあるが。」

「ぼく北海道で見たよ。」

みんなは何のことだかわからずだまってしまいました。

　ほんとうにそこはもう上の野原の入口で、きれいに刈られた草の中に一本の巨きな栗の木が立ってその幹は根もとの所がまっ黒に焦げて巨きな洞のようになり、その枝には古い縄や、切れたわらじなどがつるしてありました。

　「もう少し行ぐづどみんなして草刈ってるぞ。それがら馬の居るどごもあるぞ。」一郎は言いながら先に立って刈った草のなかの一ぽんみちをぐんぐん歩きました。

　三郎はその次に立って

　「ここには熊居ないから馬をはなして置いてもいいなあ。」と言って歩きました。

　しばらく行くとみちばたの大きななら楢の木の下に、縄で編んだ袋が投げ出してあって、沢山の草たばがあっちにもこっちにもころがっていました。

　せなかに〔約二字分空白〕をしょった二匹の馬が、一郎を見て、鼻をぷるぷる鳴らしました。

　「兄な。居るが。兄な。来たぞ。」一郎は汗を拭いながら叫びました。

　「おおい。ああい。そこに居ろ。今行ぐぞ。」

　ずうっと向うの窪みで、一郎の兄さんの声がしました。

　陽がぱっと明るくなり、兄さんがそっちの草の中から笑って出て来ました。

trunk 「幹」

shred of old rope 「古い縄」(shred: 断片)

tatters of straw sandals 「切れたわらじ」(tatter: 切れ端)

forged ahead 「ぐんぐん歩きました」、前へ進んだ

mowed grass 「刈った草」

oak trees 「楢の木」

hemp bags 麻袋

snorted 鼻を鳴らした

hollow 「窪み」

in two shakes of a lamb's tail すぐに、できるだけ早く

beaming 「笑って」、(人の顔などが) 晴れやかに、輝いて

"Thanks for comin'. You got all your friends there? They're all welcome," said his brother, looking back at them. "Take the horse back with you, okay? It's gonna cloud over later today for sure. I'm gonna stay here a bit and get this grass bundled up. You all go down to the embankment if you're gonna play. Still about twenty horses from the farm up here. But don't stray from the embankment. It's dangerous if you lose your way. I'll join you all around noon."

"We'll stick close to the embankment."

Ichiro's brother disappeared. A thin veil of clouds hung over the sky and the white mirror of the sun seemed to be tipping away from them. The grasses that hadn't yet been mowed were a sea of waves in the spiraling wind.

Ichiro walked ahead of the others on the straight path until he came to the embankment. Two logs lay where the embankment had broken away. Kosuke was about to go around them when Kasuke spoke up.

"I can lift these off any day," he said.

Kasuke took hold of an end of one of the logs and sent it tumbling down, as the others jumped over it. Some seven shiny brown horses with freely waving tails were milling about a slightly elevated place on the other side.

"Those horses are all worth more than a thousand yen a head," said Ichiro, nearing them. "They're all gonna be put in the horse races next year."

The horses trotted over to where Ichiro and the others were, as if longing for human company. They stuck their noses out as far forward as they could, hoping to get something from the boys.

「善ぐ来たな。みんなも連れで来たのが。善ぐ来た。戻りに馬こ連れでてけろな。今日ぁ午まがらきっと曇る。俺もう少し草集めて仕舞がらな、うなだ遊ばばあの土手の中さ入ってろ。まだ牧馬の馬二十疋ばかり居るがらな。」

兄さんは向うへ行こうとして、振り向いてまた言いました。

「土手がら外さ出はるなよ。迷ってしまうづど危なぃがらな。午まになったらまた来るがら。」

「うん。土手の中に居るがら。」

そして一郎の兄さんは行ってしまいました。空にはうすい雲がすっかりかかり、太陽は白い鏡のようになって、雲と反対に馳せました。風が出て来てまだ刈ってない草は一面に波を立てます。一郎はさきにたって小さなみちをまっすぐに行くとまもなくどてになりました。その土手の一とこちぎれたところに二本の丸太の棒を横にわたしてありました。耕助がそれをくぐろうとしますと、嘉助が

「おらこったなもの外せだだど。」と言いながら片っ方のはじをぬいて下におろしましたのでみんなはそれをはね越えて中に入りました。向うの少し小高いところにてかてか光る茶いろの馬が七疋ばかり集ってしっぽをゆるやかにばしゃばしゃふっているのです。

「この馬みんな千円以上するづもな。来年がらみんな競馬さも出はるのだっじゃい。」一郎はそばへ行きながら言いました。

馬はみんないままでさびしくって仕様なかったというように一郎だちの方へ寄ってきました。

そして鼻づらをずうっとのばして何かほしそうにするのです。

stray （道から）外れる、それる

tumbling down 転がり落ちる

trotted over （駆け）「寄ってきました」

"Aw," they said, putting their hands out to pet the horses, "they want salt."

Saburo, who it seemed was not used to horses, shoved his hands uneasily into his pockets.

"Look," said Etsuji, "Matasaburo's afraid of horses."

"Who's afraid of horses?" said Saburo, taking his hands out of his pockets and reaching for a horse's nose. But when the horse thrust its head toward him and put out its tongue to lick him, he suddenly turned pale and stuck his hands right back into his pockets.

"See," said Etsuji again, "Matasaburo's afraid of 'em after all."

Saburo turned beet red and just stood there fidgeting.

"Okay then," he said, "you all want to have a horse race?" None of them had a clue as to how you held a horse race.

"I've seen lots of horse races," said Saburo. "But none of these horses has a saddle so you can't ride them. So, we'll all each chase a horse, and the first one who gets to that big tree over there … see it? … he'll be the winner."

"Oh, that's fun," said Kasuke.

"If the herdsman sees us we'll be in big trouble."

"It'll be okay," said Saburo. "It'll give some practice to the horses who are racing next year."

"Great. This horse's mine."

"An' this one's mine."

"Well, I guess I gotta settle for this one."

「ははあ、塩をけろづのだな。」みんなは言いながら手を出して馬になめさせたりしましたが三郎だけは馬になれていないらしく気味悪そうに手をポケットへ入れてしまいました。

「わあ又三郎馬怖(おっか)ながるじゃい。」と悦治が言いました。

すると三郎は

「怖くなんかないやい。」と言いながらすぐポケットの手を馬の鼻づらへのばしましたが馬が首をのばして舌をべろりと出すとさあっと顔いろを変えてすばやくまた手をポケットへ入れてしまいました。

「わあい、又三郎馬怖ながるぢゃい。」悦治がまた言いました。すると三郎はすっかり顔を赤くしてしばらくもじもじしていましたが

「そんなら、みんなで競馬やるか。」と言いました。

競馬ってどうするのかとみんな思いました。

すると三郎は、

「ぼく競馬何べんも見たぞ。けれどもこの馬みんな鞍(くら)がないから乗れないや。みんなで一疋ずつ馬を追ってはじめに向うの、そら、あの巨(おお)きな樹(き)のところに着いたものを一等にしよう。」

「そいづ面白な。」嘉助が言いました。

「叱(しか)らえるぞ。牧夫に見っ附らえでがら。」

「大丈夫だよ。競馬に出る馬なんか練習をしていないといけないんだい。」三郎が言いました。

「よしおらこの馬だぞ。」

「おらこの馬だ。」

「そんならぼくはこの馬でもいいや。」

shoved 「入れて」、押し込んで、つっこんで

uneasily 「気味悪そうに」、不安そうに

thrust 「のばして」、突き出して、押し出して

saddle 「鞍」

They all lightly swatted the horses with their willow bark whips and tufts of reeds.

But the horses acted with total indifference. They just lowered their head to the ground and munched on the grass, occasionally raising their eyes as if nonchalantly taking in the scenery.

"Giddyup!" said Ichiro, whipping his horse with both hands gripping his whip.

This sent all seven horses running away with their manes lined up in the air.

"Goodee!" cried Kasuke, bolting after them.

But there was no way that this could be seen as a horse race. First of all, the horses ran absolutely neck and neck the whole way and in no way fast enough for this to be called a race. Even so, the boys were having a ball, trotting behind the horses and screaming "Giddyup … giddyup!" The horses seemed to be stopping up ahead, but the boys, though panting and out of breath, pushed on to catch up with them. Finally, the horses went around the slightly elevated place where they were before and came to the embankment that the four boys had crossed.

"The horses are getting away, they're getting away!" shouted Ichiro, turning pale. "Catch 'em, quick, don't let 'em get away!"

The horses were crossing over the embankment. They started to run again and were about to jump over the log that was still there.

"Whoa … whoa whoa whoa," said Ichiro as he ran as fast as his legs would take him, almost falling over but finally getting to where the horses were and reaching out to them. But by then two of the horses had already made it to the other side.

みんなは楊の枝や萱の穂でしゅうと言いながら馬を軽く打ちました。ところが馬はちっともびくともしませんでした。やはり下へ首を垂れて草をかいだり首をのばしてそこらのけしきをもっとよく見るというようにしているのです。

一郎がそこで両手をぴしゃんと打ち合せて、だあと言いました。すると俄かに七疋ともまるでたてがみをそろえてかけ出したのです。

「うまぁぃ。」嘉助ははね上って走りました。けれどもそれはどうも競馬にはならないのでした。第一馬はどこまでも顔をならべて走るのでしたしそれにそんなに競走するくらい早く走るのでもなかったのです。それでもみんなは面白がってだあだと言いながら一生けん命そのあとを追いました。

馬はすこし行くと立ちどまりそうになりました。みんなもすこしはあはあしましたがこらえてまた馬を追いました。するといつか馬はぐるっとさっきの小高いところをまわってさっき四人ではいって来たどての切れた所へ来たのです。

「あ、馬出はる、馬出はる。押えろ、押えろ。」

一郎はまっ青になって叫びました。じっさい馬はどての外へ出たのらしいのでした。どんどん走ってもうさっきの丸太の棒を越えそうになりました。一郎はまるであわてて「どうどうどうどう。」と言いながら一生けん命走って行ってやっとそこへ着いてまるでころぶようにしながら手をひろげたときはもう二疋はもう外へ出ていたのでした。

swatted 「軽く打ちました」、ピシャリとたたき

willow bark whips 「楊の枝」（whip: むち）

tufts of reeds 「萱の穂」

indifference 無関心

nonchalantly 平然として、何気なく

Giddyup 「だあ」、はいどう、進め

whipping 「打ち合せて」、むちで打って

manes 「たてがみ」

Goodee! 「うまぁぃ」、うわっ、うわーい。無邪気な満足感を表す

bolting 「はね上って走り」、急に駆け出して

neck and neck 「顔をならべて」。競馬で馬が首と首を並べて接戦を繰り広げている様子から、「接戦で」という意味を持つ

having a ball 「面白がって」、楽しんで

trotting behind （走って後を）「追いました」

pushed on 「こらえて」

Whoa 「どうどう」

"Get over here!" hollered Ichiro out of breath, putting the log back where it was. "Quick, we gotta catch 'em!"

The boys ran like the devil, avoiding the logs, but the two horses had stopped on the other side of the embankment and were yanking grass out of the ground with their teeth.

"Don't rush, take it slow and easy," said Ichiro, grabbing one horse by the bit.

But when Kasuke and Saburo tried to get a hold on the bit of the other horse, it bolted as if alarmed and ran at full speed south along the embankment.

"The horse's getting away!" shouted Ichiro at the top of his lungs in the direction of where his brother was. "It's getting away … away!"

Kasuke and Saburo ran after the horse, and this time it really looked like it was trying to get away. It galloped through grasses that were as tall as it was, raising and lowering its head and never about to stop. Kasuke's legs got all numb and he hadn't a clue where the horse was now. Everything went all blue around him, he got dizzier and dizzier and, in the end, fell right into the tall grass. The last thing he caught a glimpse of was the red mane of the horse and the white shirt of Saburo running after it. He was flat on his back. He looked up at the sky. The sky was like a radiant white pinwheel and the dull gray clouds in it were streaming far into the distance. He heard a loud clanging noise, finally got up and, breathing in fits and starts, started to walk in the direction that the horse ran in.

「早ぐ来て押えろ。早ぐ来て。」一郎は息も切れるように叫びながら丸太棒をもとのようにしました。三人は走って行って急いで丸太をくぐって外へ出ますと二疋の馬はもう走るでもなくどての外に立って草を口で引っぱって抜くようにしています。

「そろそろど押えろよ。そろそろど。」と言いながら一郎は一ぴきのくつわについた札のところをしっかり押えました。嘉助と三郎がもう一疋を押えようとそばへ寄りますと馬はまるで愕いたようにどてへ沿って一目散に南の方へ走ってしまいました。

「兄な馬ぁ逃げる、馬ぁ逃げる。兄な。馬逃げる。」とうしろで一郎が一生けん命叫んでいます。三郎と嘉助は一生けん命馬を追いました。

ところが馬はもう今度こそほんとうに遁げるつもりらしかったのです。まるで丈ぐらいある草をわけて高みになったり低くなったりどこまでも走りました。

嘉助はもう足がしびれてしまってどこをどう走っているのかわからなくなりました。

それからまわりがまっ蒼になって、ぐるぐる廻り、とうとう深い草の中に倒れてしまいました。馬の赤いたてがみとあとを追って行く三郎の白いシャッポが終りにちらっと見えました。

嘉助は、仰向けになって空を見ました。空がまっ白に光って、ぐるぐる廻り、そのこちらを薄い鼠色の雲が、速く速く走っています。そしてカンカン鳴っています。

嘉助はやっと起き上って、せかせか息しながら馬の行った方に歩き出しました。

＜段落の途中で改ページをしています＞

---

yanking 「引っぱって」

bit 「くつわ」、馬はみ

galloped 「走りました」、（馬などが）駆けて

numb 「しびれて」

flat on his back 「仰向けになって」

radiant 「光って」、輝いて

pinwheel 風車

clanging noise 「カンカン」（鳴る音）

in fits and starts 「せかせか」、発作的に、断続的に

There was a kind of opening in the grass where, it seemed, the horse and Saburo had gone, and he thought, laughing to himself, "Sure, the horse's scared and has stopped somewhere in his tracks." He followed through that opening in the grass, but before he went even a hundred steps the opening branched out into two other openings where honeysuckle and strangely tall thistles were growing. He had totally lost his bearings and didn't know which way was which.

"Hullo!" he hollered.

"Hullo!" shouted Saburo from somewhere.

Hearing this, Kasuke forged ahead down an opening in the middle. But he just came upon places that were overgrown and steep inclines that a horse could never walk over.

The sky turned fiercely dark, layer by layer, and the surroundings were enveloped, by degrees, in a dim mist. A cold wind began to traverse the grasses, and both the clouds and the mist fragmented, rushing straight into his eyes.

"Ah, I'm really in trouble now," thought Kasuke. "It's an omen of one bad thing after another that's gonna happen."

And he was right. In a flash, the opening that the horse had gone through disappeared in the grass. Kasuke's heart raced. "We're in for it. Everything's going to go to the devil now," he thought.

The grasses bent at their stalks, clicking and clacking as they rustled in the strong wind, the fog grew milky and thick, and his clothes hung on him like a damp blanket.

"Ichiro, Ichiro," screamed Kasuke at the top of his voice. "Get over here!"

honeysuckle スイカ
ズラ。「おとこえし」は、
スイカズラ科の多年草で、
オミナエシに似ているが姿
はより逞しい

thistles 「薊」

lost his bearings 「ど
れがどれやら一向わからな
くなってしまいました」、
(lose one's bearings:
方向がわからなくなる)

steep inclines 「急な
所」、急斜面

fiercely 「たいへん」、猛
烈に、ひどく

enveloped 覆われて、
包まれて

by degree 少しずつ、
徐々に

traverse 「渡り」、横切
り

fragmented 「切れ切れ
になって」、断片化した

omen of... 〜の前兆、
前触れ

one bad thing after
another 一難去ってま
た一難

In a flash 「俄かに」、い
きなり、一瞬で

We're in for it 「悪く
なった」、まずいことになっ
た

stalks 「からだ」、茎

clicking and clacking
「パチパチ」、カチカチ、カ
チャカチャ

damp blanket 湿った
毛布

草の中には、今馬と三郎が通った痕らしく、かすかな路
のようなものがありました。嘉助は笑いました。そし
て、

（ふん。なあに、馬どこかで、こわくなってのっこり立っ
てるさ。）と思いました。

そこで嘉助は、一生懸命それを跡けて行きました。と
ころがその路のようなものは、まだ百歩も行かないうち
に、おとこえしや、すてきに背の高い薊の中で、二つに
も三つにも分れてしまって、どれがどれやら一向わから
なくなってしまいました。嘉助はおういと叫びました。

おうとどこかで三郎が叫んでいるようです。

思い切って、そのまん中のを進みました。けれどもそ
れも、時々断れたり、馬の歩かないような急な所を横様
に過ぎたりするのでした。

空はたいへん暗く重くなり、まわりがぼうっと霞んで
来ました。冷たい風が、草を渡りはじめ、もう雲や霧が、
切れ切れになって眼の前をぐんぐん通り過ぎて行きまし
た。

（ああ、こいつは悪くなって来た。みんな悪いことはこ
れから集ってやって来るのだ。）と嘉助は思いました。全
くその通り、俄に馬の通った痕は、草の中で無くなって
しまいました。

（ああ、悪くなった、悪くなった。）嘉助は胸をどきど
きさせました。

草がからだを曲げて、パチパチ言ったり、さらさら鳴っ
たりしました。霧が殊に滋くなって、着物はすっかりし
めってしまいました。

嘉助は咽喉一杯叫びました。

「一郎、一郎こっちさ来う。」

But there was no reply. Tiny dark cold globules of mist, like chalk dust falling off a blackboard, danced through the air, a hush fell over everything, all there was around him was misery and gloom, and all that could be heard was the trickling and dripping of water sliding off the grass.

Kasuke turned back to join Ichiro and the others as fast as he could. But the place he was running through was not the same as before. First of all, there were way too many thistles in the way and jagged rocks hiding below the grass that weren't there before. Besides that, a huge valley that no one had ever talked about appeared right before his eyes. The pampas grass rustled and the space in front of him just vanished into the fog like a bottomless ravine.

The fronds of the pampas grass lengthened their myriad thin fingers into the wind, furiously waving as if to say, "Ah, West … ah, East … ah, West … ah, South … ah, West…."

Kasuke was mortified and he turned sideways, rushing back from where he came, coming across a narrow black path through the grass that was made by thousands of horses' hoofs. He let out a little laugh and raced down the path for all he was worth. But he couldn't trust the path because it kept getting narrower down to five inches then wider up to three feet and then going what seemed like around in circles, before branching off into the haze in several directions when it reached a burnt chestnut tree with spreading branches at the top. It was probably a place where wild horses gathered, because he could see what looked like a corral through the fog.

ところが何の返事も聞えません。黒板から降る白墨の粉のような、暗い冷たい霧の粒が、そこら一面踊りまわり、あたりが俄にシインとして、陰気に陰気になりました。草からは、もう雫の音がポタリポタリと聞えて来ます。

嘉助はもう早く、一郎たちの所へ戻ろうとして急いで引っ返しました。けれどもどうも、それは前に来た所とは違っていたようでした。第一、薊があんまり沢山ありましたし、それに草の底にさっき無かった岩かけが、度々ころがっていました。そしてとうとう聞いたこともない大きな谷が、いきなり眼の前に現われました。すすきが、ざわざわざわっと鳴り、向うの方は底知れずの谷のように、霧の中に消えているではありませんか。

風が来ると、芒の穂は細い沢山の手を一ぱいのばして、忙しく振って、

「あ、西さん、あ、東さん。あ西さん。あ南さん。あ、西さん。」なんて言っている様でした。

嘉助はあんまり見っともなかったので、目を瞑って横を向きました。そして急いで引っ返しました。小さな黒い道が、いきなり草の中に出て来ました。それは沢山の馬の蹄の痕で出来上っていたのです。嘉助は、夢中で、短い笑い声をあげて、その道をぐんぐん歩きました。

けれども、たよりのないことは、みちのはばが五寸ぐらいになったり、また三尺ぐらいに変ったり、おまけに何だかぐるっと廻っているように思われました。そして、とうとう、大きなてっぺんの焼けた栗の木の前まで来た時、ぼんやり幾つにも岐れてしまいました。

そこは多分は、野馬の集まり場所であったでしょう、霧の中に円い広場のように見えたのです。

globules of mist 「霧の粒」(globule: しずく、小滴)

chalk dust 「白墨の粉」

hush 「シイン」、静寂

misery and gloom 「陰気に陰気に」(misery: 惨めな、gloom: 陰気な)

trickling and dripping 「ポタリポタリ」(trickle、drip: ぼたぼた落ちる、滴る)

jagged rocks 「岩かけ」

pampas grass 「すすき」

fronds 「穂」、葉

myriad 「沢山の」、無数の

mortified 「見っともなかった」、恥ずかしい思いをした

horses' hoofs 「馬の蹄」

for all he was worth 「ぐんぐん」、全力で、懸命に

corral 馬の囲い

Kasuke, crestfallen, started to retrace his steps on the black path. Fronds and tufts that he had never seen before were all around, swaying in silence, and when a strong wind began to blow, the body of grass around him bowed down, as if on signal from somewhere or other to make room for him. The sky creaked with light.

A huge black object shaped like a house appeared out of the fog right before his eyes. Kasuke stood there for a time disbelieving his own eyes, but it definitely looked like a house. He took one reluctant step after the other toward it until he realized that it was a huge frigid black boulder. The sky swung and swayed, revolving around itself, and the grass shook off all its droplets in one fell jolt.

"If we go wrong here and descend from the other side of the field," thought Kasuke, half saying it in a whisper, "both Matasaburo and I are goners."

Then he screamed out …

"Ichiro, Ichiro, you there? ICHIRO!"

It brightened up again, all the grasses heaved a happy sigh of relief, and he clearly heard words that someone had once said to him.

"The child of the electrician at Isado had his hands and feet tied by a giant woodsman."

That's when the black path vanished again and everything around went quiet as the grave and a ferociously strong wind swirled in. The sky fluttered in light, like a flag, and sparks crackled and burned in the air.

Kasuke finally fell into the grass and was soon dead to the world.

crestfallen 「がっかりして」

retrace 「戻り」、引き返す

Fronds and tufts 「草穂」

creaked 「キインと鳴って」、キーキーと音を立てて

frigid 「冷たい」、極寒の

shook off 「払いました」(shake off: 振り払う)

in one fell jolt 「バラッと」。in one fell swoop をもじった言い回し。宮沢賢治はしばしば作品のなかでそのような言葉遊びを行った(in one fell swoop: 一気に、突然)

goners 死者

heaved (息を)吐いた、(胸などを)脹らませた

electrician 「電気工夫」

giant woodsman 「山男」

quiet as the grave (墓場のように)「しいんと」

dead to the world 「ねむって」、ぐっすり眠り込んで

　嘉助はがっかりして、黒い道をまた戻りはじめました。知らない草穂が静かにゆらぎ、少し強い風が来る時は、どこかで何かが合図をしてでも居るように、一面の草が、それ来たっとみなからだを伏せて避けました。

　空が光ってキインキインと鳴っています。それからすぐ眼の前の霧の中に、家の形の大きな黒いものがあらわれました。嘉助はしばらく自分の眼を疑って立ちどまっていましたが、やはりどうしても家らしかったので、こわごわもっと近寄って見ますと、それは冷たい大きな黒い岩でした。

　空がくるくるくるっと白く揺らぎ、草がバラッと一度に雫を払いました。

　(間違って原の向う側へ下りれば、又三郎もおれももう死ぬばかりだ。)と嘉助は、半分思う様に半分つぶやくようにしました。それから叫びました。

　「一郎、一郎、居るが。一郎。」

　また明るくなりました。草がみな一斉に悦びの息をします。

　「伊佐戸の町の、電気工夫の童ぁ、山男に手足ぃ縛らえてたふうだ。」といつか誰かの話した語が、はっきり耳に聞えて来ます。

　そして、黒い路が、俄に消えてしまいました。あたりがほんのしばらくしいんとなりました。それから非常に強い風が吹いて来ました。

　空が旗のようにぱたぱた光って翻えり、火花がパチパチッと燃えました。嘉助はとうとう草の中に倒れてねむってしまいました。

It all seemed like things that happened somewhere far away.

Matasaburo had remained silent. He was looking up at the sky with outstretched legs and was now wearing a glass mantle over his usual gray jacket. His shoes too were made of gleaming glass. The blue shadow of a chestnut tree fell on his shoulders, and his own shadow, in turn, fell blue into the grass. And the wind whistled higher and higher.

Matasaburo was neither speaking nor smiling. He was merely gazing up at the sky with his thin lips clamped shut like a vice. All of a sudden he flew up in the air just like that, his glass mantle glittering and gleaming with him.

Kasuke suddenly opened his eyes. The gray fog was sailing far far away, and the horse was standing solidly right in front of him, looking askance as if wary of him. Kasuke bolted up and held him by the name tag, as Saburo came from behind with his colorless lips shut tight. Kasuke shook like a leaf.

"Hullo!" called Ichiro's brother from a bank of fog, as thunder rolled over them.

"Hullo!" cried Ichiro. "Kasuke, you there? Kasuke!"

"Hey, I'm here, I'm here. Ichiro, hullo!"

Before he knew it Ichiro and his brother were standing in front of him, and he started bawling his eyes out.

"We looked for you everywhere," said Ichiro's brother, cradling the horse's neck with a practiced hand while skillfully attaching the bit in its mouth. "We were worried about your safety. Oh, gosh, you're soaking wet."

"Let's get outta here."

そんなことはみんなどこかの遠いできごとのようでした。

もう又三郎がすぐ眼の前に足を投げだしてだまって空を見あげているのです。いつかいつもの鼠いろの上着の上にガラスのマントを着ているのです。それから光るガラスの靴をはいているのです。

又三郎の肩には栗の木の影が青く落ちています。又三郎の影はまた青く草に落ちています。そして風がどんどんどんどん吹いているのです。又三郎は笑いもしなければ物も言いません。ただ小さな唇を強そうにきっと結んだまま黙ってそらを見ています。いきなり又三郎はひらっとそらへ飛びあがりました。ガラスのマントがギラギラ光りました。ふと嘉助は眼をひらきました。灰いろの霧が速く速く飛んでいます。

そして馬がすぐ眼の前にのっそりと立っていたのです。その眼は嘉助を怖れて横の方を向いていました。

嘉助ははね上って馬の名札を押えました。そのうしろから三郎がまるで色のなくなった唇をきっと結んでこっちへ出てきました。嘉助はぶるぶるふるえました。

「おうい。」霧の中から一郎の兄さんの声がしました。雷もごろごろ鳴っています。

「おおい、嘉助。居るが。嘉助。」一郎の声もしました。嘉助はよろこんでとびあがりました。

「おおい。居る、居る。一郎。おおい。」

一郎の兄さんと一郎が、とつぜん、眼の前に立ちました。嘉助は俄かに泣き出しました。

「探したぞ。危ながったぞ。すっかりぬれだな。どう。」一郎の兄さんはなれた手付きで馬の首を抱いてもってきたくつわをすばやく馬のくちにはめました。

「さあ、あべさ。」

with outstretched legs 「足を投げ出して」

glass mantle 「ガラスのマント」

merely 「ただ」

clamped shut like a vice （万力のように）「きっと結んだ」

looking askance 横目で見て

wary of... 「～を怖れて」、警戒して

cradling 「抱いて」

with a practiced hand 「なれた手付きで」

"You must've been really spooked, Matasaburo," said Ichiro to Saburo.

But Saburo just stood there with his lips clamped shut like before.

They all followed Ichiro's brother as he climbed up two gentle slopes and took the big black path for a while. A couple of lightning flashes dimly lit the white sky and the smell of burning grass filled the air that flowed in billows, like smoke, through the fog.

"Grandpa," shouted Ichiro, "we found him, we found him. We're all here!"

"Goodness, I was worried, worried sick," said his grandfather, standing against a bank of fog. "Thank goodness. Oh, Kasuke, you must be freezin'. C'mon, get on in here."

Ichiro's grandfather was just like a grandfather to Kasuke too.

There was a little enclosure made of grasses at the root of a tall halfburnt chestnut tree, with a crackling red fire ablaze in it. Ichiro's brother tied the horse, who was neighing, to the trunk of an oak tree.

"Aw, poor kid, you must've cried yer eyes out. That boy's the miner's boy, ain't he. Now, all of you, dig into these dumplings. C'mon, don't be shy. I'll grill these ones here for ya. So, where on earth did you all get to?"

"Down to the place that leads to Sasanagane," answered Ichiro's brother.

"Aw, it's not safe down there, not safe at all. We've lost horses and people down there. Now, Kasuke, eat up that dumpling. You, too, kid, have one. Come on, don't leave any."

"Grandpa, should I leave the horse here?" asked Ichiro's brother.

「又三郎びっくりしたべぁ。」一郎が三郎に言いました。三郎がだまってやっぱりきっと口を結んでうなずきました。

みんなは一郎の兄さんについて緩い傾斜を、二つ程昇り降りしました。それから、黒い大きな路について、暫らく歩きました。

稲光が二度ばかり、かすかに白くひらめきました。草を焼く匂がして、霧の中を煙がほっと流れています。

一郎の兄さんが叫びました。

「おじいさん。居だ、居だ。みんな居だ。」

おじいさんは霧の中に立っていて、

「ああ心配した、心配した。ああ好がった。おお嘉助。寒がべぁ、さあ入れ。」と言いました。嘉助は一郎と同じようにやはりこのおじいさんの孫なようでした。

半分に焼けた大きな栗の木の根もとに、草で作った小さな囲いがあって、チョロチョロ赤い火が燃えていました。

一郎の兄さんは馬を楢の木につなぎました。

馬もひひんと鳴いています。

「おおむぞやな。な。何ぼが泣いだがな。そのわろは金山掘りのわろだな。さあさあみんな、団子たべろ。食べろ。な、今こっちを焼ぐがらな。全体どこ迄行ってだった。」

「笹長根の下り口だ。」と一郎の兄さんが答えました。

「危ぃがった。危ぃがった。向うさ降りだら馬も人もそれっ切りだったぞ。さあ嘉助。団子喰べろ。このわろもたべろ。さあさあ、こいづも食べろ。」

「おじいさん。馬置いでくるが。」と一郎の兄さんが言いました。

spooked 「びっくりした」、驚いた

billows （煙や炎などの）うねり、渦

worried sick （とても）「心配した」

bank of fog 霧峰

ablaze 「燃えて」、燃え立って

neighing いななく

miner's boy 「金山掘りのわろ」、金山掘りの息子

dig into these dumplings 「団子喰べろ」

風の又三郎　69

"Hmmm. When the herdsman gets here he's bound to make a fuss. Hold on here a bit longer, will ya? It's bound to clear up soon. Aw, I was worried sick. I went down the mountain to look for ya. Yup, well, anyway, thank goodness, that's all I gotta say. Rain's clearin' up too."

"Weather was pretty good this mornin'."

"Yup, looks like it'll hold. But the damn rain's leakin' in."

Ichiro's brother left. The roof of the enclosure was swishing and humming in the wind. The grandfather looked up at it with a big smile, as Ichiro's brother returned.

"Grandpa, it's all bright out. The rain's stopped."

"Hmm, right. Now all of ya get yerself close to the fire. I'm goin' out to cut some more grass."

Bright rays of sunshine cleaved the fog. The sun had sailed on to the west. Radiant bands of fog lingered in the air, like wax. Droplets glittered as they fell from blades of grass and all the leaves and stalks and flowers sucked up the sun near the end of day. The blue fields far away in the west had stopped their crying out and were now beaming, and the chestnut tree in the distance was giving off a light blue aura.

They were all exhausted as they followed Ichiro down to the field they had come from. Saburo, his lips together as before, separated from the others when they came to the spring and went off by himself to his father's cottage.

"He's gotta be the god of the winds," said Kasuke, walking along. "I mean, the child of the god of the winds. He and his dad are livin' up here."

"You're wrong, he's not," insisted Ichiro.

「うんうん。牧夫来るどまだやがましがらな。したども
も少し待で。またすぐ晴れる。ああ心配した。俺も虎こ
山の下まで行って見で来た。はあ、まんつ好がった。雨
も晴れる。」

「今朝ほんとに天気好がったのにな。」

「うん、また好ぐなるさ。あ、雨漏って来たな。」

　一郎の兄さんが出て行きました。天井がガサガサガサ
ガサ言います。おじいさんが、笑いながらそれを見上げ
ました。

　兄さんがまたはいって来ました。

「おじいさん。明るぐなった。雨ぁ霽れだ。」

「うんうん。そうが。さあみんなよっく火にあだれ、お
らまた草刈るがらな。」

　霧がふっと切れました。陽の光がさっと流れて入りま
した。その太陽は、少し西の方に寄ってかかり、幾片か
の蠟のような霧が、逃げおくれて仕方なしに光りました。

　草からは雫がきらきら落ち、総ての葉も茎も花も、今
年の終りの陽の光を吸っています。

　はるかな西の碧い野原は、今泣きやんだようにまぶし
く笑い、向うの栗の木は、青い後光を放ちました。みん
なはもう疲れて一郎をさきに野原をおりました。湧水の
ところで三郎はやっぱりだまってきっと口を結んだまま
みんなに別れてじぶんだけお父さんの小屋の方へ帰って
行きました。

　帰りながら嘉助が言いました。

「あいづやっぱり風の神だぞ。風の神の子っ子だぞ。あ
そこさ二人して巣食ってるんだぞ。」

「そだないよ。」一郎が高く言いました。

herdsman 「牧夫」

bound to... 必ず〜す
る、〜するに違いない

leakin' in 「漏って来た」

swishing and
humming 「ガサガサガ
サガサ」（swish：（風など
が）シュッと鳴る、hum：
ブンブン鳴る）

cleaved the fog 霧を
切り裂いた

lingered 「逃げおくれ
て」、なかなか消えず、い
つまでも残り

light blue aura 「青い
後光」

5 September

The next day it had stopped raining by morning and by the second hour of school the sky was getting brighter and brighter. By the time the ten-minute recess came in the third hour you could see blue patches of sky etched between the clouds. Layers of bright white cirrocumulus cloud were sailing swiftly toward the east, where a vapor of cloud remained and, rising up from the reeds and the chestnut trees, blanketed the mountains.

"Wanna go pick grapes after class?" whispered Kosuke to Kasuke.

"You bet I do! Maybe Matasaburo wants to come with us," said Kasuke.

"No! Don't let Saburo know about that spot."

"I'll go with you," said Saburo, not having heard what Kosuke had just said. "I picked heaps of grapes in Hokkaido. My mum pickled up two barrels of them."

"If you're goin' grape pickin', take me too!" piped in Shokichi, a second-grade pupil.

"No way! There's no way we'd tell you where it is. I found this new place last year myself."

They all couldn't wait till school ended. Six of them—Ichiro, Kasuke, Sataro, Kosuke, Etsuji and Matasaburo—went upriver from the school to where there was a house with a straw roof behind a small tobacco field. The bottom leaves had already been picked from the tobacco bushes, and the boys thought that the blue-green stalks, all lined up like trees in a forest, looked weird. "What's going on with these leaves?" blurted out Saburo, ripping off a leaf and showing it to Ichiro.

九月五日

　次の日は朝のうちは雨でしたが、二時間目からだんだん明るくなって三時間目の終りの十分休みにはとうとうすっかりやみ、あちこちに削ったような青ぞらもできて、その下をまっ白な鱗雲がどんどん東へ走り、山の萱からも栗の木からも残りの雲が湯気のように立ちました。

　「下ったら葡萄蔓とりに行がないが。」耕助が嘉助にそっと言いました。

　「行ぐ行ぐ。又三郎も行がないが。」嘉助がさそいました。耕助は、

　「わあい、あそご三郎さ教えるやないじゃ。」と言いましたが三郎は知らないで、

　「行くよ。ぼくは北海道でもとったぞ。ぼくのお母さんは樽へ二つっ漬けたよ。」と言いました。

　「葡萄とりにおらも連れでがないが。」二年生の承吉も言いました。

　「わがないじゃ。うなどさ教えるやないじゃ。おら去年な新らしいどご目附だじゃ。」

　みんなは学校の済むのが待ち遠しかったのでした。五時間目が終ると、一郎と嘉助が佐太郎と耕助と悦治と又三郎と六人で学校から上流の方へ登って行きました。少し行くと一けんの藁やねの家があって、その前に小さなたばこ畑がありました。たばこの木はもう下の方の葉をつんであるので、その青い茎が林のようにきれいにならんでいかにも面白そうでした。

　すると三郎はいきなり、

　「何だい、この葉は。」と言いながら葉を一枚むしって一郎に見せました。すると一郎はびっくりして、

etched 「削った」
cirrocumulus cloud
「鱗雲」
vapor 「湯気」、蒸気
pickled 「漬けた」
blurted out 思わず口
走った

"Hey, Matasaburo," said Ichiro, turning pale and alarmed. "If you rip off leaves the Tobacco Monopoly Bureau will skin you alive. What did you go and do that for, Matasaburo?!"

They all turned on Saburo.

"Hell, the bureau records every single leaf they got here. Don't come to me."

"And don't come to me either."

"And not to me either."

"I didn't know that, I just took it," said Saburo hesitantly, blushing and somewhat miffed as he waved the leaf about.

They all looked toward the house, terrified that someone had seen them. But it seemed that no one was in the house, which they could see through the steam puffing up from the field.

"That's little Kisuke's house, the first-grade boy," said Kasuke to calm everyone down.

Kosuke had been really against Saburo and everyone tagging along to the thicket where the grapes grew that he had discovered.

"It's not good enough that you didn't know," he said nastily to Saburo. "So, you gotta put it back were you tore it off from and pay the damages."

"Well, if that's the case," said Matasaburo, trying to find the right words after a long pause, "I'll just put it back down here."

He gently laid the leaf at the root of the bush.

"Okay, let's get outta here," said Ichiro, strutting ahead.

They all followed him, except for Kosuke, who turned to Saburo.

「わあ、又三郎、たばごの葉とるづど専売局にうんと叱られるぞ。わあ、又三郎何してとった。」と少し顔いろを悪くして言いました。みんなも口々に言いました。

「わあい。専売局でぁ、この葉一枚ずつ数えで帖面さつけでるだ。おら知らないぞ。」

「おらも知らないぞ。」

「おらも知らないぞ。」みんな口をそろえてはやしました。

すると三郎は顔をまっ赤にして、しばらくそれを振り廻わして何か言おうと考えていましたが、

「おら知らないでとったんだい。」と怒ったように言いました。

みんなは怖そうに、誰か見ていないかというように向うの家を見ました。たばこばたけからもうもうとあがる湯気の向うで、その家はしいんとして誰も居たようではありませんでした。

「あの家一年生の小助の家だじゃい。」嘉助が少しなだめるように言いました。ところが耕助ははじめからじぶんの見附けた葡萄藪へ、三郎だのみんなあんまり来て面白くなかったもんですから、意地悪くもいちど三郎に言いました。

「わあ、又三郎なんぼ知らないたってわがないんだじゃ。わあい、又三郎もどの通りにしてまゆんだであ。」

又三郎は困ったようにしてまたしばらくだまっていましたが、

「そんなら、おいらここへ置いてくからいいや。」と言いながらさっきの木の根もとへそっとその葉を置きました。すると一郎は、

「早くあべ。」と言って先にたってあるきだしましたのでみんなもついて行きましたが、耕助だけはまだ残って、

Tobacco Monopoly Bureau （たばこ）「専売局」

skin you alive 「うんと叱られる」

miffed 「怒ったように」、むっとして

tagging along ついて行く

nastily 「意地悪く」

"It's all on your head, Matasaburo," he said, before catching up with the others. "That's your leaf under there."

They climbed part way up the mountain on a narrow path running through the weeds and reeds, with chestnut trees dotting the hollows on the south side of the path, below it a big thicket overgrown with grape vines.

"I found this place first," said Kosuke. "So you can all take just a handful each."

"I'll pick chestnuts instead," said Saburo, picking up a stone and throwing it at one of the branches, bringing down a burr.

He peeled the burr with a stick and took out two chestnuts that were still white, as the others were busying themselves by the vines. But Kosuke was soon off to another thicket, passing under the chestnut tree, when all of a sudden a big splash of water fell right onto him, and it looked like he'd been dunked in the river from his shoulders down his back. He looked up in shock to see Matasaburo on a branch with a funny little smile on his lips, wiping his face on his shirt cuff. "Hey, Matasaburo," said Kosuke, bitterly, "what the hell d'ya think you're doin'?!"

"The wind came up," said Saburo, sniggering.

Kosuke walked away, went to another thicket and began to pick grapes. He picked much more than he himself could handle, stuffing some into his mouth, which now was purple and bloated.

"Well," said Ichiro, "I think I'll call it a day with this much."

"I'm not through yet here," said Kosuke.

「ほう、おら知らないぞ。ありゃ、又三郎の置いた葉、あすごにあるじゃい。」なんて言っているのでしたがみんながどんどん歩きだしたので耕助もやっとついて来ました。

みんなは萱の間の小さなみちを山の方へ少しのぼりますと、その南側に向いた窪みに栗の木があちこち立って、下には葡萄がもくもくした大きな藪になっていました。

「こごおれ見っ附だのだがらみんなあんまりとるやないぞ。」耕助が言いました。

すると三郎は、

「おいら栗の方をとるんだい。」といって石を拾って一つの枝へ投げました。青いいがが一つ落ちました。

又三郎はそれを棒きれで剝いて、まだ白い栗を二つとりました。みんなは葡萄の方へ一生けん命でした。

そのうち耕助も一つの藪へ行こうと一本の栗の木の下を通りますと、いきなり上から雫が一ぺんにざっと落ちてきましたので、耕助は肩からせなかから水へ入ったようになりました。耕助は愕いて口をあいて上を見ましたら、いつか木の上に又三郎がのぼっていて、なんだか少しわらいながらじぶんも袖ぐちで顔をふいていたのです。

「わあい、又三郎何する。」耕助はうらめしそうに木を見あげました。

「風が吹いたんだい。」三郎は上でくつくつわらいながら言いました。

耕助は樹の下をはなれてまた別の藪で葡萄をとりはじめました。もう耕助はじぶんでも持てないくらいあちこちへためていて、口も紫いろになってまるで大きく見えました。

「さあ、この位持って戻らないが。」一郎が言いました。

「おら、もっと取ってぐじゃ。」耕助が言いました。

dotting 「あちこち立って」、点在して

grape vines 葡萄のつる

burr 「いが」

dunked in 「水へはいった」、水に浸った

sniggering 「くつくつわらいながら」、せせら笑いながら

bloated 「大きく」、膨れた、むくんだ

Just then Kosuke's head was drenched in big drops of cold water. Taken by surprise again he looked up to the branches above him. This time Saburo wasn't there at all, but he did glimpse Saburo's gray elbow on the other side of the tree. Saburo was still sniggering at him and it made him furious.

"Hey, Matasaburo! You throwin' water on people again?"

"No, it was from the wind."

Everyone found this hilarious … except, that is, Kosuke, who didn't look happy and was staring daggers at Saburo.

"You went and shook the tree, Matasaburo."

Again the others found this hilarious.

"Listen good, Matasaburo. There's no place in this world for the likes of you!"

"All right, little Kosuke," said Matasaburo in a mean voice. "Well, excuse me for living."

Kosuke was so furious that he wasn't able to say what he wanted to and couldn't think of anything new to say either.

"Listen good, Matasaburo, and watch yer step!" he shrieked. "We don't need wind like you comin' into our world, you hear?"

"Well, then, I am truly sorry," he said, blinking over and over and feeling a bit sorry. "What can I do? You're just so awful to me."

But this in no way assuaged Kosuke's anger, and he repeated what he said for the third time.

"Hear me, Matasaburo! There's no place in the world for any wind. Get it?"

そのとき耕助はまた頭からつめたい雫をざあっとかぶりました。耕助はまたびっくりしたように木を見上げましたが今度は三郎は樹の上には居ませんでした。

　けれども樹の向う側に三郎の鼠_{ねずみ}いろのひじも見えていましたし、くつくつ笑う声もしましたから、耕助はもうすっかり怒ってしまいました。

　「わあい又三郎、まだひとさ水掛げだな。」

　「風が吹いたんだい。」

　みんなはどっと笑いました。

　「わあい又三郎、うなそごで木ゆすったけぁなあ。」

　みんなはどっとまた笑いました。

　すると耕助はうらめしそうにしばらくだまって三郎の顔を見ながら、

　「うあい又三郎汝_{うな}などあ世界になくてもいなあぃ」

　すると又三郎はずるそうに笑いました。

　「やあ耕助君失敬したねえ。」

　耕助は何かもっと別のことを言おうと思いましたがあんまり怒ってしまって考え出すことが出来ませんでしたのでまた同じように叫びました。

　「うあい、うあいだが、又三郎、うなみだいな風など世界中になくてもいいなあ、うわあい」

　「失敬したよ。だってあんまりきみもぼくへ意地悪をするもんだから。」又三郎は少し眼をパチパチさせて気の毒そうに言いました。けれども耕助のいかりは仲々解けませんでした。そして三度同じことをくりかえしたのです。

　「うわい、又三郎風などあ世界中に無くてもいな、うわい」

drenched in...　「〜をざあっとかぶり」、びしょぬれになり

glimpse　ちらりと見える

staring daggers at...　「うらめしそうに〜を見ながら」、〜をにらみつけながら

assuaged　和らげた、癒した

no place for wind in the world　「風などあ世界中に無くてもいな」（no place for...: 〜の出る場所ではない）

"What do you mean by no place for wind in the world?" said Matasaburo, sniggering again and now drawn into the discussion, raising a finger in the air like a teacher. "Okay, then. Would you please itemize what you want to say, one by one? Get it?"

Kosuke felt like he was being tested and he really didn't like it one bit.

"You are just up to mischief all the time," he said, gritting his teeth. "You ruin everyone's umbrellas."

"And what else, what else?" said Matasaburo, clearly enjoying this.

"An' you break apart trees and turn them topsy-turvy."

"Okay, and what else?"

"You rip apart people's homes."

"Okay, what else, what else do I do?"

"You snuff out people's lights."

"Okay, is that all? Is that all I do? Come on."

"You send people's hats flying."

"Uh-huh, and what else, what else do I do?"

"You send people's umbrellas flying too."

"What else, what else?"

"You … you … you bring down telephone poles."

"Tell me more, tell me more, tell me more."

"And you take people's roofs off people's houses."

"Ha ha ha, roofs should be included in the earlier part about the houses. Okay, so do you have anything else? Come on, what else?"

"What else? You … you put out people's lamps."

"Ha ha ha, lamps should be included in the part about the lights. So, are you through? Hey, come on, what else can you come up with?"

すると又三郎は少し面白くなった様でまたくつくつ笑いだしてたずねました。

　「風が世界中に無くってもいいってどう言うんだい。いいと箇条をたてていってごらん。そら」又三郎は先生みたいな顔つきをして指を一本だしました。耕助は試験の様だしつまらないことになったと思って大へん口惜《くや》しかったのですが仕方なくしばらく考えてから言いました。

　「汝《うな》など悪戯《いたずら》ばりさな、傘《かさ》ぶっ壊《か》したり。」

　「それからそれから」又三郎は面白そうに一足進んで言いました。

　「それがら樹折《き》ったり転覆《おっけあ》したりさな」

　「それから、それからどうだい」

　「家もぶっ壊《か》さな。」

　「それからそれから、あとはどうだい」

　「あかしも消さな、」

　「それから、あとは？　それからあとは？　どうだい」

　「シャップもとばさな」

　「それから？　それからあとは？　あとはどうだい。」

　「笠《かさ》もとばさな。」

　「それからそれから」

　「それがら　うう電信ばしらも倒さな」

　「それから？　それから？　それから？」

　「それがら屋根もとばさな」

　「アアハハハ屋根は家のうちだい。どうだいまだあるかい。それから、それから？」

　「それだがら、うう、それだがらランプも消さな。」

　「アハハハハハ、ランプはあかしのうちだい。けれどそれだけかい。え、おい。それから？　それからそれから。」

drawn into... 「少し面白くなった」、～に引き込まれた

itemize 「箇条をたてて」、明細を挙げて

mischief 「悪戯」、悪さ

gritting his teeth 歯を食いしばって

break apart ぶっ壊す、打ち壊す、ばらばらにする

turn... topsy-turvy 「転覆したり」、～を逆さまにしたり

rip apart ぶっ壊す、引き裂く、ばらばらにする

snuff out... （火などを）消す

telephone poles 「電信ばしら」

Kosuke was stumped. He had said just about everything and he couldn't come up with anything else.

"Come on, what else? Eh? You can do it. What else?" said Matasaburo, with a finger in the air, thoroughly enjoying himself.

"You … you smash up windmills," said Kosuke finally, his face reddening from ear to ear.

Matasaburo found this funnier than all the others and burst out laughing. All the others followed suit, giggling and chortling and guffawing.

"So, you finally got to the windmills," said Matasaburo, ceasing to laugh. "There isn't a windmill that doesn't love a wind. There may be the odd time that they are broken by the wind, but much more often it helps them go around. I tell you, windmills look up to the wind. And besides, the way you listed those things a moment ago was really weird. 'You … you … you' … you kept repeating that. And then you got to the windmills at the end. Ah, it really makes me crack up!"

And having said that, Matasaburo howled with laughter until his eyes were running with tears. As for Kosuke, he gradually stopped thinking about how angry and bothered he was and started to laugh himself.

"Kosuke," said Matasaburo, now in a good mood, "sorry about the mischief."

"Well now, how about we set off," said Ichiro, handing Matasaburo five bunches of grapes. Matasaburo shared two white chestnuts each with the other boys and they all walked down the sloping path together, separating and going to their own home in the end.

耕助はつまってしまいました。大抵もう言ってしまったのですからいくら考えてももう出ませんのでした。又三郎はいよいよ面白そうに指を一本立てながら

「それから？　それから？　ええ？　それから」と言うのでした。

耕助は顔を赤くしてしばらく考えてからやっと答えました。

「風車もぶっ壊《か》さな。」

すると又三郎はこんどこそはまるで飛び上って笑ってしまいました。みんなも笑いました。笑って笑って笑いました。

又三郎はやっと笑うのをやめて言いました。

「そらごらんとうとう風車などを言っちゃったろう。風車なら風を悪く思っちゃいないんだよ、勿論《もちろん》時々こわすこともあるけれども、廻してやる時の方がずっと多いんだ。風車ならちっとも風を悪く思っていないんだ。それに第一お前のさっきからの数えようはあんまりおかしいや。うう、うう、でばかりいたんだろう。おしまいにとうとう風車なんか数えちゃった、ああおかしい」又三郎はまた泪《なみだ》の出るほど笑いました。耕助もさっきからあんまり困ったために怒っていたのもだんだん忘れて来ました、そしてつい又三郎と一しょに笑い出してしまったのです。すると又三郎もすっかりきげんを直して、

「耕助君、いたずらをして済まなかったよ」と言いました。

「さあそれでぁ行ぐべな。」と一郎は言いながら又三郎にぶどうを五ふさばかりくれました。又三郎は白い栗をみんなに二つずつ分けました。そしてみんなは下のみちまでいっしょに下りてあとはめいめいのうちへ帰ったのです。

---

thoroughly enjoying himself 「いよいよ面白そうに」、存分に楽しみながら

smash up　ぶっ壊す、たたき壊す

windmills 「風車」

followed suit　後に続いた、追随した

chortling 「面白くて」声を立てて笑う

guffawing　大笑いする

ceasing to laugh 「笑うのをやめて」（cease to...：〜することをやめる、〜しなくなる）

odd time 「時々」、時折

look up to...　〜を尊敬する、〜を仰ぐ

7 September

A mantle of fog hung over the morning of the next day and the mountain behind the school was virtually lost in the haze. But once again the day began to brighten up around the time of the second hour and soon the sky was clear and the sun was beating down so that by noon, when the littlest children went home, it was as hot as any day in the middle of summer.

By early afternoon the teacher was having to wipe the sweat off his brow in front of the blackboard. It was so muggy that the fourth-grade pupils doing their penmanship and the fifth- and sixth-grade pupils their drawing were all but dropping off with a pencil in their hand.

They all filed down to the river right after class.

"Hey, Matasaburo," said Kasuke, walking in front of Matasaburo. "Wanna join us for a swim? These days everyone from the littlest up goes."

They weren't going where they went before. This time they went to a stream flowing off the right side of the river where there was quite a wide dry bed and further down a huge gleditsia tree grew out of the side of a cliff.

"Hey there!" hollered some half-naked little boys who had arrived before them, waving both hands in the air.

Ichiro and the others ran like the wind through the silk trees on the dry riverbed and, in a flash, they had stripped down to their loin cloth and were splashing about in the water, crouching down and spurting water at each other, and lining up on an angle to swim to the other side. The boys who were there earlier swam after them. Saburo was the last to take off his clothes and get into the water. He swam for a bit then laughed out loud.

九月七日

　次の朝は霧がじめじめ降って学校のうしろの山もぼんやりしか見えませんでした。ところが今日も二時間目ころからだんだん晴れて間もなく空はまっ青になり日はかんかん照ってお午になって三年生から下が下ってしまうとまるで夏のように暑くなってしまいました。

　ひるすぎは先生もたびたび教壇で汗を拭き四年生の習字も五年生六年生の図画もまるでむし暑くて書きながらうとうとするのでした。

　授業が済むとみんなはすぐ川下の方へそろって出掛けました。嘉助が

　「又三郎水泳びに行がないが。小さいやづど今ころみんな行ってるぞ。」と言いましたので又三郎もついて行きました。

　そこはこの前上の野原へ行ったところよりもも少し下流で右の方からも一つの谷川がはいって来て少し広い河原になりそのすぐ下流は巨きなさいかちの樹の生えた崖になっているのでした。

　「おおい。」とさきに来ているこどもらがはだかで両手をあげて叫びました。一郎やみんなは、河原のねむの木の間をまるで徒競走のように走っていきなりきものをぬぐとすぐどぶんどぶんと水に飛び込んで両足をかわるがわる曲げてだぁんだぁんと水をたたくようにしながら斜めにならんで向う岸へ泳ぎはじめました。

　前に居たこどもらもあとから追い付いて泳ぎはじめました。

　又三郎もきものをぬいでみんなのあとから泳ぎはじめましたが、途中で声をあげてわらいました。

mantle of fog　一面の霧、濃霧

virtually　ほとんど、実質

in the haze　かすんで、霧に隠れて

beating down　「かんかん照って」、（太陽が）照りつけて

muggy　「むし暑く」

dropping off　「うとうとする」、まどろむ

all filed down to the river　「川下の方へそろって出掛けました」（file: 列をつくって進む）

gleditsia tree　「さいかちの樹」。サイカチ属の落葉高木。果実の莢は、石鹸の代わりに使われた

silk trees　「ねむの木」。マメ科ネムノキ亜科の落葉高木。夜になると葉が閉じて眠りにつくように見えることが由来

stripped down to their loin cloth　服を脱ぐ（loin cloth: ふんどし）

spurting water　「水をたたく」、水を噴き出す

"Hey, Matasaburo," shouted Ichiro from the other bank, shivering with purple lips and slicking his hair down like a seal's, "what's so funny?"

"This water's freezing," said Matasaburo, shivering as he came out of water.

"So, what were you laughin' at, Matasaburo?" asked Ichiro for a second time.

"At the way you swam," said Matasaburo, now all giggles. "I mean, why do you slosh your legs around like that?"

"Hey, huh?" said Ichiro, feeling awkward, but then, picking up a white stone, adding, "Wanna play find-the-stone?"

"I do, I do," shouted all the children on the bank.

"Okay, so I'll go above where that tree is and drop it down."

Ichiro easily climbed halfway up the cliff to where the gleditsia was.

"Okay, it's comin' down. Ready, set, go!" he said, dropping the white stone with a splash into the deep pool in the river.

They all plunged headfirst into the river, each one determined to get to the stone first, diving right down to the bottom like bluish-white otters, aiming for the stone. But not all of them could make it to the bottom, and some had to come up for air, as a mist streamed in waves over the river. Matasaburo had been closely watching the others dive down, and, after they returned to the surface in happy spirits, he himself plunged in, as four adults who had stripped to the waist by the silk trees on the far bank were coming toward him carrying a net.

すると向う岸についた一郎が髪をあざらしのようにして唇（くちびる）を紫にしてわくわくふるえながら、

「わあ又三郎、何（な）してわらった。」と言いました。又三郎はやはりふるえながら水からあがって

「この川冷たいなあ。」と言いました。

三郎は、

「おまえたちの泳ぎ方はおかしいや。なぜ足をだぶだぶ鳴らすんだい。」と言いながらまた笑いました。

「うわあい、」と一郎は言いましたが何だかきまりが悪くなったように

「石取りさないが。」と言いながら白い円い石をひろいました。

「するする」こどもらがみんな叫びました。

おれそれでぁあの木の上がら落とすがらな。と一郎は言いながら崖（がけ）の中ごろから出ているさいかちの木へするする昇って行きました。そして

「さあ落すぞ、一二三。」と言いながら、その白い石をどぶーんと淵（ふち）へ落しました。みんなはわれ勝に岸からまっさかさまに水にとび込んで青白いらっこのような形をして底へ潜ってその石をとろうとしました。けれどもみんな底まで行かないに息がつまって浮びだして来て、かわるがわるふうとそらへ霧をふきました。

又三郎はじっとみんなのするのを見ていましたが、みんなが浮んできてからじぶんもどぶんとはいって行きました。けれどもやっぱり底まで届かずに浮いてきたのでみんなはどっと笑いました。そのとき向うの河原のねむの木のところを大人が四人、肌ぬぎになったり網をもったりしてこっちへ来るのでした。

すると一郎は木の上でまるで声をひくくしてみんなに叫びました。

---

slicking his hair down like a seal's 「髪をあざらしのようにして」（slick... down: ～をなでつける、seal: アザラシ）

slosh 「だぶだぶ鳴らす」、（水中で）バシャバシャ動かす

feeling awkward 「きまりが悪く」、気恥ずかしく

find-the-stone 「石取り」

plunged headfirst into the river 「まっさかさまに水にとび込んで」（headfirst: まっさかさまに、無鉄砲に）

bluish-white otters 「青白いらっこ」

stripped to the waist 「肌ぬぎになった」。和服の袖から腕を抜いて、上半身をあらわにすること

"Hey, everyone, they're gonna be blasting!" hollered Ichiro in a low voice from his place just above where the tree was. "Play dumb and just leave the stone and get downriver right away!"

All of the children did their best to not look at the adults, continuing to swim downstream together. Ichiro surveyed the scene with his hands on his cheeks and plunged head over heels into the pool, making a beeline through the water until catching up with the others.

They all stood in the shallows downstream from the pool.

"Just play dumb, everyone," said Ichiro.

They all just picked up grindstones, chased wagtails and pretended not to be the least concerned about any blasting.

Shosuke, who was a miner downriver from there, peered about from the bank of the pool for a while then suddenly sat down on the pebbles and crossed his legs. He methodically took a tobacco pouch from around his waist, filled his long-stem pipe and smoked. He reached into his work vest and pulled out an object.

"They're gonna blast, they're gonna blast!" cried all the children.

But Ichiro waved his hands, gesturing for them to stop screaming. Shosuke put the little bowl of his pipe to the object, as a man behind him entered the water to prepare the net. Shosuke, as calm as could be, rose and, with one foot in the water, flung the object to a point in the river right below the gleditsia tree. At that there was an awful boom, the water there swelled up and for a time a ringing lingered in the air. That's when the other adults got into the water.

「おお、発破<ruby>発破<rt>はっぱ</rt></ruby>だぞ。知らないふりしてろ。石とりやめで早ぐみんな<ruby>下流<rt>しも</rt></ruby>ささがれ。」

　そこでみんなは、なるべくそっちを見ないふりをしながらいっしょに<ruby>下流<rt>しも</rt></ruby>の方へ泳ぎました。一郎は、木の上で手を額にあてて、もう一度よく見きわめてから、どぶんと<ruby>逆<rt>さかさ</rt></ruby>まに淵へ飛びこみました。それから水を<ruby>潜<rt>くぐ</rt></ruby>って、一ぺんにみんなへ追いついたのです。

　みんなは、淵の<ruby>下流<rt>しも</rt></ruby>の、瀬になったところに立ちました。

　「知らないふりして遊んでろ。みんな。」一郎が言いました。みんなは、<ruby>砥石<rt>といし</rt></ruby>をひろったり、せきれいを追ったりして、発破のことなぞ、すこしも気がつかないふりをしていました。

　すると向うの淵の岸では、下流の坑夫をしていた庄助が、しばらくあちこち見まわしてから、いきなりあぐらをかいて、砂利の上へ座ってしまいました。それからゆっくり、腰からたばこ入れをとって、きせるをくわえて、ぱくぱく煙をふきだしました。奇体だと思っていましたら、また腹かけから、何か出しました。

　「発破だぞ、発破だぞ。」とみんな叫びました。一郎は、手をふってそれをとめました。庄助は、きせるの火を、しずかにそれへうつしました。うしろに居た一人は、すぐ水に入って、網をかまえました。庄助は、まるで落ちついて、立って一あし水にはいると、すぐその持ったものを、さいかちの木の下のところへ投げこみました。するとまもなく、ぼぉというようなひどい音がして、水はむくっと盛りあがり、それからしばらく、そこらあたりがきぃんと鳴りました。向うの大人たちは、みんな水へ入りました。

blasting 「発破」、爆破

making a beeline 「一ぺんに」、一直線に

crossed his legs 「あぐらをかいて」

methodically 「ゆっくり」、念入りに

long-stem pipe 「きせる」

work vest 「腹かけ」。職人などがつける作業着で、胸から腹にかけて覆い、細い布紐を背中で十文字に交差させてとめる

flung 「投げこみました」、放り投げた

ringing lingered 「きぃんと鳴りました」

"They're floatin' past. Grab 'em!" said Ichiro.

Kosuke grabbed a brown sculpin the size of a pinkie that was floating belly up down the river, and right behind him Kasuke with a beet-red face shouted like he was slurping melon when he snagged a carp about six inches long. All the other children were catching fish too, jumping up and down in the water with glee.

"Pipe down, pipe down!" said Ichiro.

Several adults, some with shirts on and some without, came running from the bleached dry riverbed, and a man in a see-through shirt came galloping bareback headlong toward them, just like in the movies. The adults were attracted by the explosion.

"Slim pickin's," said Shosuke, folding his arms over his chest and looking at the fish that the children were gripping onto.

"You can have these back," said Matasaburo, standing next to Shosuke and putting two medium-size carp on the ground for throwing back into the river.

"Who's this kid, eh? Some weirdo?" said Shosuke, staring Matasaburo up and down.

Matasaburo went back to the others without saying anything. Shosuke gave him a dirty look and all the others just laughed. Then Shosuke went upriver and the other adults followed him, including the man in the see-through shirt, who was still on horseback. Kosuke swam to the place where Saburo had put the two fish down and brought them back to where the other children were, and they all had a good laugh.

"Let's scatter the small fry!" shouted Kasuke, hopping up and down on the sandbar.

「さあ、流れて来るぞ。みんなとれ。」と一郎が言いました。まもなく、耕助は小指ぐらいの茶いろなかじかが、横向きになって流れて来たのをつかみましたしそのうしろでは嘉助が、まるで瓜をすするときのような声を出しました。それは六寸ぐらいある鮒をとって、顔をまっ赤にしてよろこんでいたのです。それからみんなとってわあわあよろこびました。

「だまってろ、だまってろ。」一郎が言いました。

そのとき、向うの白い河原を、肌ぬぎになったり、シャツだけ着たりした大人が、五六人かけて来ました。そのうしろからは、ちょうど活動写真のように、一人の網シャツを着た人が、はだか馬に乗って、まっしぐらに走って来ました。みんな発破の音を聞いて、見に来たのです。

庄助は、しばらく腕を組んでみんなのとるのを見ていましたが、

「さっぱり居なぃな。」と言いました。すると又三郎がいつの間にか庄助のそばへ行っていました。

そして中位の鮒を二疋「魚返すよ。」といって河原へ投げるように置きました。すると庄助が

「何だこの童ぁ、きたいなやづだな。」と言いながらじろじろ又三郎を見ました。

又三郎はだまってこっちへ帰ってきました。庄助は変な顔をしてみています。みんなはどっとわらいました。

庄助はだまって、また上流へ歩きだしました。ほかのおとなたちもついて行き網シャツの人は、馬に乗って、またかけて行きました。耕助が泳いで行って三郎の置いて来た魚を持ってきました。みんなはそこでまたわらいました。

「発破かけだら、雑魚撒かせ。」嘉助が、河原の砂っぱの上で、ぴょんぴょんはねながら、高く叫びました。

sculpin 「かじか」

pinkie 「小指」

belly up （死んだ魚が）
腹を上にして

slurping melon 「瓜を
すする」（slurp: 大きな音
を立てて飲食する）

snagged 「とって」、
さっとつかんで、捕らえて

carp 「鮒」

Pipe down 「だまって
ろ」、静かにしろ

bleached dry
riverbed 白い河原
（bleached: 漂白された、
真っ白の）

Slim pickin's 「さっぱ
り居ない」、雀の涙、ちょっ
ぴりの量

scatter 「撒かせ」、ばら
撒け

small fry 「雑魚」

sandbar 「砂っぱ」、砂
州

They all made a little circular tank with rocks in the shallow water to keep the fish alive and from swimming away, then ran to the cliff face and started to climb up to the gleditsia tree. The sun was blazing hot now, the silk trees looked all droopy like they did in the middle of summer, and the sky was like a bottomless pool.

"Oh no, someone's bustin' up our fish tank!" shouted one of the children.

Sure enough, a man with a weirdly pointy nose, dressed in a suit and straw sandals, was stirring up the fish with what looked like a stick.

"He's from the Monopoly Bureau, the Monopoly Bureau," said Sataro.

"Hey, Matasaburo," said Kasuke, "he's come to get you for rippin' off that tobacco leaf."

"So what, I'm not scared," said Matasaburo, biting down on his lip.

"Let's all surround Matasaburo," said Ichiro. "Make a circle around him."

They all sat in a circle on the branches of the gleditsia tree with Matasaburo on a branch in the middle.

The man started to slosh his way right along the bank toward the boys.

"He's coming, he's coming!"

They held their breath. But the man apparently didn't have his sights on Matasaburo at all and just walked right past them, stepping into the shallows next to the pool. He stopped in the middle of the river and walked back and forth, washing the dirt off his sandals and cloth leggings. The children felt less anxious about him but didn't take to him either.

みんなは、とった魚を、石で囲んで、小さな生州をこしらえて、生き返っても、もう遁げて行かないようにして、また上流のさいかちの樹へのぼりはじめました。ほんとうに暑くなって、ねむの木もまるで夏のようにぐったり見えましたし、空もまるで、底なしの淵のようになりました。

そのころ誰かが、

「あ、生州、打壊すとこだぞ。」と叫びました。見ると、一人の変に鼻の尖った、洋服を着てわらじをはいた人が、手にはステッキみたいなものをもって、みんなの魚を、ぐちゃぐちゃ掻きまわしているのでした。

「あ、あいづ専売局だぞ。専売局だぞ。」佐太郎が言いました。

「又三郎、うなのとった煙草の葉めっけだんだぞ。うな、連れでぐさ来たぞ。」嘉助が言いました。

「何だい、こわくないや。」又三郎はきっと口をかんで言いました。

「みんな又三郎のごと囲んでろ囲んでろ。」と一郎が言いました。

そこでみんなは又三郎をさいかちの樹のいちばん中の枝に置いてまわりの枝にすっかり腰かけました。

その男はこっちへびちゃびちゃ岸をあるいて来ました。

「来た来た来た来た来たっ。」とみんなは息をころしました。ところがその男は、別に又三郎をつかまえる風でもなくみんなの前を通りこしてそれから淵のすぐ上流の浅瀬をわたろうとしました。それもすぐに河をわたるでもなく、いかにもわらじや脚絆の汚なくなったのを、そのまま洗うというふうに、もう何べんも行ったり来たりするもんですから、みんなはだんだん怖くなくなりましたがその代り気持ちが悪くなってきました。そこで、とうとう、一郎が言いました。

circular tank 「生州」

droopy 「ぐったり」、しなだれた

bustin' up... 「打壊す」、粉々に破壊する

fish tank 「生州」

pointy nose 「鼻の尖った」

straw sandals 「わらじ」

rippin' off もぎ取る、盗む

felt less anxious about him but didn't take to him either その男を不審に思う気持ちは和らいだが、好きにはなれなかった（didn't take to...: ～を好きではない、～を気に入らない）

"I'm gonna yell first," said Ichiro, "and then I want you all to yell on my count. Got it? 'Don't dirty up the river! We'll tell our teacher on you!' Okay … one, two, three!"

"DON'T DIRTY UP THE RIVER! WE'LL TELL OUR TEACHER ON YOU!"

The man looked their way and spoke, but the children couldn't catch what he said.

Once again they screamed out what they had screamed out before.

"You people here drink this water, do you?" said the man with the pointy nose, pursing his lips like someone puffing out cigarette smoke.

"Don't dirty up the river! We'll tell our teacher on you!"

"So, a man's not allowed to walk in the river, huh?" he said, a bit miffed.

"Don't dirty up the river! We'll tell our teacher on you!"

The man continued to ford the river at a leisurely pace, as if to hide the fact that he was somewhat rattled, then climbed up the blue clay and red pebble bluff on an angle, just like an Alpine mountain climber, disappearing into the tobacco field above.

"What's the big deal?" said Matasaburo, jumping straight off the branch and splashing into the pool. "He wasn't here to get me at all."

All the others followed one by one, feeling both a little sorry for the man and Matasaburo but also a little drained inside. They swam to the dry riverbed, wrapped the fish in hand towels and took them home.

「お、おれ先に叫ぶから、みんなあとから、一二三で叫ぶこだ。いいか。
　あんまり川を濁すなよ、
　いつでも先生言うでないか。一、二ぃ、三。」
「あんまり川を濁すなよ、
　いつでも先生言うでないか。」
　その人は、びっくりしてこっちを見ましたけれども、何を言ったのか、よくわからないというようすでした。そこでみんなはまた言いました。
「あんまり川を濁すなよ、
　いつでも先生、言うでないか。」
　鼻の尖った人は、すぱすぱと、煙草を吸うときのような口つきで言いました。
「この水呑むのか、ここらでは。」
「あんまり川をにごすなよ、
　いつでも先生言うでないか。」
　鼻の尖った人は、少し困ったようにして、また言いました。
「川をあるいてわるいのか。」
「あんまり川をにごすなよ、
　いつでも先生言うでないか。」
　その人は、あわてたのをごまかすように、わざとゆっくり、川をわたって、それから、アルプスの探検みたいな姿勢をとりながら、青い粘土と赤砂利の崖をななめにのぼって、崖の上のたばこ畑へはいってしまいました。
　すると又三郎は
「何だいぼくを連れにきたんじゃないや。」と言いながらまっ先にどぶんと淵へとび込みました。
　みんなも何だかその男も又三郎も気の毒なような、おかしながらんとした気持ちになりながら、一人ずつ木からはね下りて、河原に泳ぎついて、魚を手拭につつんだり、手にもったりして、家に帰りました。

puffing out... （タバコなどの煙を）吐き出す

ford the river 「川をわたって」（ford:（浅瀬を）渡る）

rattled 「あわてた」、混乱した、動揺した

blue clay 「青い粘土」

red pebble bluff 「赤砂利の崖」

Alpine mountain climber 「アルプスの探検」、アルプスの登山者

feeling... a little drained inside 「がらんとした気持ちになり」

hand towels 「手拭い」

風の又三郎　95

8 September

The next morning all the children were having fun in the yard before class, hanging off the bars and playing hide-the-stick. Sataro arrived a bit late, carrying a basket with something in it.

"What'cha got? What'cha got?" said all the children, rushing up to him and peeking into the basket.

Sataro put his sleeve over the top of the basket and hurried off to the cave in the rock behind the school. The children ran after him. Ichiro took one look in the basket and turned as white as a ghost. Sataro was carrying prickly-ash powder for poisoning and killing fish, and, like blasting them, you can get arrested for using that. After hiding it in the weeds by the cave, Sataro went back to the yard without a care in the world. And that's all the children talked about in breathy whispers until it was time for class.

By about ten o'clock it was as hot as blazes like the day before. All the children could think about was the end of the school day. When the fifth hour was finished at two, they all flew out of there. Sataro went back to furtively covering the top of his basket with his sleeve, followed by Kosuke, as they all traipsed down to the dry riverbed. Matasaburo went with Kasuke. They brushed past the silk trees that were giving off a fusty smell, like gas at a town festival, till they got to the cliff face by the pool where the gleditsia tree was.

九月八日

　次の朝授業の前みんなが運動場で鉄棒にぶら下ったり棒かくしをしたりしていますと、少し遅れて佐太郎が何かを入れた笊をそっと抱えてやって来ました。

　「何だ。何だ。何だ。」とすぐみんな走って行ってのぞき込みました。すると佐太郎は袖でそれをかくすようにして急いで学校の裏の岩穴のところへ行きました。みんなはいよいよあとを追って行きました。一郎がそれをのぞくと思わず顔いろを変えました。それは魚の毒もみにつかう山椒の粉で、それを使うと発破と同じように巡査に押えられるのでした。ところが佐太郎はそれを岩穴の横の萱の中へかくして、知らない顔をして運動場へ帰りました。

　そこでみんなはひそひそ時間になるまでひそひそその話ばかりしていました。

　その日も十時ごろからやっぱり昨日のように暑くなりました。みんなはもう授業の済むのばかり待っていました。二時になって五時間目が終ると、もうみんな一目散に飛びだしました。佐太郎もまた笊をそっと袖でかくして耕助だのみんなに囲まれて河原へ行きました。又三郎は嘉助と行きました。みんなは町の祭のときの瓦斯のような匂のむっとする、ねむの河原を急いで抜けて、いつものさいかち淵に着きました。すっかり夏のような立派な雲の峰が、東でむくむく盛りあがり、さいかちの木は青く光って見えました。

prickly-ash powder
「山椒の粉」

get arrested 「押えられる」、逮捕される

as hot as blazes （ものすごく）「暑く」

furtively 「そっと」、こっそりと、ひそかに

traipsed down ぶらぶら歩いた

brushed past... 「～を急いで抜けて」、～を通り過ぎて、～をすり抜けて

giving off a fusty smell 「むっとする」（においを放つ）

An immense bank of summer cloud was towering over the eastern horizon and the gleditsia tree was shining blue. They all quickly slipped out of their clothes and stood by the side of the pool.

"Stand in a straight line, okay?" said Sataro, looking right into Ichiro's eyes. "If you see a fish floatin' up, swim out and grab it. Just catch it, that's all. Got it?"

The little children were jumping with joy and, with bright red faces, they pushed and shoved each other to get a good place around the pool. Pekichi and a few of the others were already in the water waiting at a spot below the gleditsia tree. Sataro, totally pleased with himself, went to the shallows upriver and dipped the basket in the water over and over again, as they all stared into the pool in silence. Matasaburo was not looking at the water at all but had set his sight on a black bird that was flying over the bank of cloud. As for Ichiro, he was plopped down on the dry riverbed knocking rocks together. But no matter how much time passed not a single fish came floating up to the surface.

Sataro stood straight up and down peering into the water with a very serious expression on his face. They had all seen about ten fish floating up after the blasting the day before and continued to wait there without saying a word for the same thing to happen. But again, not one fish showed up on the surface.

"They're just not floatin' up, are they," shouted Kosuke.

Sataro gave a start, but it didn't stop him from peering constantly into the water.

"Not even one's there," said Pekichi from below the tree.

They all began gabbing away and jumping into the pool.

"How about playin' tag?" said Sataro, crouching by the side of the water and feeling pretty ashamed of himself.

みんな急いで着物をぬいで、淵の岸に立つと、佐太郎が一郎の顔を見ながら言いました。

「ちゃんと一列にならべ。いいか。魚浮いて来たら、泳いで行ってとれ。とった位与るぞ。いいか。」

小さなこどもらは、よろこんで顔を赤くして、押しあったりしながら、ぞろっと淵を囲みました。ペ吉だの三四人は、もう泳いで、さいかちの木の下まで行って待っていました。

佐太郎、大威張りで、上流の瀬に行って笊をじゃぶじゃぶ水で洗いました。みんなしんとして、水をみつめて立っていました。又三郎は水を見ないで、向うの雲の峰の上を通る黒い鳥を見ていました。一郎も河原に座って石をこちこち叩いていました。ところがそれからよほどたっても、魚は浮いて来ませんでした。

佐太郎は大へんまじめな顔で、きちんと立って水を見ていました。昨日発破をかけたときなら、もう十疋もとっていたんだと、みんなは思いました。またずいぶんしばらくみんなしんとして待ちました。けれどもやっぱり、魚は一ぴきも浮いて来ませんでした。

「さっぱり魚、浮かばないな。」耕助が叫びました。佐太郎はびくっとしましたけれども、まだ一心に水を見ていました。

「魚さっぱり浮ばないな。」ペ吉が、また向うの木の下で言いました。するともうみんなは、がやがやと言い出して、みんな水に飛び込んでしまいました。

佐太郎は、しばらくきまり悪そうに、しゃがんで水を見ていましたけれど、とうとう立って、

「鬼っこしないか。」と言った。

immense bank of summer cloud 「夏のような立派な雲の峰」（immense: 巨大な、bank of clouds: 入道雲）

towering over... 「盛りあがり」、〜の上にそびえ

shallows 「瀬」、浅瀬

plopped down （どっかり）「座って」

"Yeah, let's play!" they all said, raising their hand in scissors or rock or paper out of the water to decide who goes first, with those in water too deep to stand swimming to a shallower place so they could join in.

Ichiro came from the dry riverbed and put his hand up too. He set the blue soggy clay place under the bluff that the weird man with the pointy nose had climbed up as the home base. If you got to there before the person who was "it" did, you were safe. Anyone who got tagged before was "it." They then began to play a pared down version of "rock paper scissors" without the scissors. But Etsuji went and put out his two fingers for scissors, causing the others to break out into catcalls and make him "it." Etsuji ran about the dry riverbed until his lips turned purple. He touched Kisaku and now there were two who were "it." They all ran helter-skelter over the sandbar and around the pool, tagging and being tagged by each other. In the end, Matasaburo too became "it." He soon caught up with Kichiro, as all the others looked on from home base below the tree.

「する、する。」みんなは叫んで、じゃんけんをするために、水の中から手を出しました。泳いでいたものは、急いでせいの立つところまで行って手を出しました。一郎も河原から来て手を出しました。そして一郎は、はじめに、昨日あの変な鼻の尖った人の上って行った崖の下の、青いぬるぬるした粘土のところを根っこにきめました。そこに取りついていれば、鬼は押えることができないというのでした。それから、はさみ無しの一人まけかちで、じゃんけんをしました。ところが、悦治はひとりはさみを出したので、みんなにうんとはやされたほかに鬼になった。悦治は、唇を紫いろにして、河原を走って、喜作を押えたので、鬼は二人になりました。それからみんなは、砂っぱの上や淵を、あっちへ行ったり、こっちへ来たり、押えたり押えられたり、何べんも鬼っこをしました。

　しまいにとうとう、又三郎一人が鬼になりました。又三郎はまもなく吉郎をつかまえました。みんなは、さいかちの木の下に居てそれを見ていました。すると又三郎が、

raising their hand in scissors or rock or paper 「じゃんけんをするために……手を出しました」

home base 「根っこ」、ホームベース

"it" 「鬼」

tagged （鬼ごっこで）つかまる、押さえられる

helter-skelter 「あっちへ行ったり、こっちへ来たり」、右往左往

"Kichiro," said Matasaburo, "you should chase everyone from upriver. You understand?"

Kichiro opened his mouth, spread his arms out and chased everyone over the blue clay earth. They all got ready to jump into the pool, except for Ichiro, who climbed up a willow tree. But Kichiro's feet had got all muddied in the clay and he slipped and tumbled down in front of everyone. They all yelled and screamed as they hurdled over Kichiro and plunged into the water or dashed for home base.

"Matasaburo, get over here!" said Kasuke with his mouth wide open and his arms outstretched, trying to fool him.

"If that's how you're going to play," said Matasaburo, clearly angered, "just watch me."

Matasaburo was determined this time. He splashed right into the water and swam with all his might toward Kasuke. His red hair splashed around and his lips turned purple from being in the water, so much so that all the other children were alarmed. For one thing, the place that was set as home base was much too cramped for all of them to get to safety there and the ground was like a slippery plate. Four or five children below had to hold onto someone above or they would slip and plop right into the pool. Only Ichiro, who was at the highest point, was calm and collected. The others were involved in a discussion, racking their brain as to what to do. Matasaburo, kicking and splashing, was getting close to them.

「吉郎君、きみは上流から追って来るんだよ、いいか。」
と言いながら、じぶんはだまって立って見ていました。
吉郎は、口をあいて手をひろげて、上流から粘土の上を
追って来ました。みんなは淵へ飛び込む支度をしました。
一郎は楊の木にのぼりました。そのとき吉郎が、あの
上流の粘土が、足についていたためにみんなの前ですべっ
てころんでしまいました。みんなは、わあわあ叫んで、
吉郎をはねこえたり、水に入ったりして、上流の青い粘
土の根に上ってしまいました。

「又三郎、来。」嘉助は立って、口を大きくあいて、手
をひろげて、又三郎をばかにしました。すると又三郎は、
さっきからよっぽど怒っていたと見えて、

「ようし、見ていろよ。」と言いながら、本気になって、
ざぶんと水に飛び込んで、一生けん命、そっちの方へ泳
いで行きました。

又三郎の髪の毛が赤くてばしゃばしゃしているのにあ
んまり永く水につかって唇もすこし紫いろなので子ども
らは、すっかり恐がってしまいました。第一、その粘土
のところはせまくて、みんながはいれなかったのにそれ
に大へんつるつるすべる坂になっていましたから、下の
方の四五人などは、上の人につかまるようにして、やっ
と川へすべり落ちるのをふせいでいたのでした。一郎だ
けが、いちばん上で落ち着いて、さあ、みんな、とか何
とか相談らしいことをはじめました。みんなもそこで、
頭をあつめて聞いています。又三郎は、ぼちゃぼちゃ、
もう近くまで行きました。

hurdled over 「はねこ
えた」

gave a start 「びくっ
としました」

gabbing away 「がや
がやと言い」（gab: 無駄
話をする、おしゃべりをす
る）

tag 「鬼っこ」、鬼ごっこ

feeling pretty
ashamed of himself
「きまり悪そうに」
（ashamed of oneself:
自分を恥じる）

determined 「本気に
なって」

with all his might 「一
生けん命」

cramped 「せまくて」、
窮屈で

slip and plop 「すべり
落ちる」（plop: ドブンと
落ちる）

calm and collected
「落ち着いて」

racking their brain
「頭をあつめて」（rack
one's brain: 知恵を絞
る）

They were all huddled together whispering to each other when Matasaburo started splashing them with both his arms. They did their best to flap their arms about trying to keep dry, but the wet clay started to slip and slide down, falling apart as it did. Matasaburo sent even more sheets of water their way.

The result was that they all came tumbling down with the clay. Matasaburo did his best to catch some of them and Ichiro pitched in too. Only Kasuke went around to the river and swam away. Matasaburo swam after him and caught him, grabbing his arms and pulling him around several times. But it looked like Kasuke was choking. He had swallowed a lot of water and was trying to spray some out of his mouth.

"I've had enough," he said. "I'm not goin' to play tag anymore."

All the littler children jumped onto the pebbles. Matasaburo remained alone under the gleditsia tree.

All of a sudden the sky was filled with black clouds, the willow tree shone strangely white, and the grasses and weeds on the mountains dimmed and darkened. Everything they could see had taken on an indescribably terrifying air. Soon thunder was rumbling about the fields on the mountains, where what sounded like a landslide was in progress, a sudden shower was drenching them and the wind was whistling and whirring in the air. The water in the pool started whirling around ferociously and you couldn't tell the waves from the rocks.

All the children picked up their clothes from the dry riverbed and started to run under the silk trees. Even Matasaburo seemed scared for the first time. He jumped into the water where the gleditsia tree was and started to swim in their direction. Then … they all heard someone say …

みんなは、ひそひそはなしています。すると又三郎は、いきなり両手で、みんなへ水をかけ出した。みんながばたばた防いでいましたら、だんだん粘土がすべって来て、なんだかすこうし下へずれたようになりました。又三郎はよろこんで、いよいよ水をはねとばしました。するとみんなは、ぼちゃんぼちゃんと一度にすべって落ちました。又三郎は、それを片っぱしからつかまえました。一郎もつかまりました。嘉助がひとり、上をまわって泳いで遁げましたら、又三郎はすぐに追い付いて、押えたほかに、腕をつかんで、四五へんぐるぐる引っぱりまわしました。嘉助は、水を呑んだと見えて、霧をふいて、ごぼごぼむせて、

「おいらもうやめた。こんな鬼っこもうしない。」と言いました。小さな子どもらはみんな砂利に上ってしまいました。又三郎は、ひとりさいかちの樹の下に立ちました。

ところが、そのときはもう、そらがいっぱいの黒い雲で、楊も変に白っぽくなり、山の草はしんしんとくらくなりそこらは何とも言われない、恐ろしい景色にかわっていました。

そのうちに、いきなり上の野原のあたりで、ごろごろごろと雷が鳴り出しました。と思うと、まるで山つなみのような音がして、一ぺんに夕立がやって来ました。風までひゅうひゅう吹きだしました。淵の水には、大きなぶちぶちがたくさんできて、水だか石だかわからなくなってしまいました。みんなは河原から着物をかかえて、ねむの木の下へ遁げこみました。すると又三郎も何だかはじめて怖くなったと見えてさいかちの木の下からどぼんと水へはいってみんなの方へ泳ぎだしました。すると誰ともなく

huddled together 集まった、群がった

flap their arms 「ばたばた防いで」

choking 「むせて」

indescribably 「何とも言われない」

landslide 「山つなみ」、山崩れ

ferociously ひどく、恐ろしく

Rain, pitter-patter, Rain-Saburo
Wind, howl-bellow, Mata-Saburo

And they all joined in …

Rain, pitter-patter, Rain-Saburo
Wind, howl-bellow, Mata-Saburo

Matasaburo was in a panic. He jumped right out of the pool as if something was pulling down on his leg and ran for dear life, shivering and trembling, to where the others were.

"Is it you who just shouted out now?" he asked.

"Not us, no, not us," they all cried in unison.

"Not us," said Pekichi, stepping out.

Matasaburo, feeling really awkward and uncomfortable, looked back at the river, tightening his pale lips as he always did.

"What's going on?" he said, shaking as before.

All the children went to their home until they thought it had cleared up.

「雨はざっこざっこ雨三郎
　風はどっこどっこ又三郎」
と叫んだものがありました。みんなもすぐ声をそろえて叫びました。
「雨はざっこざっこ雨三郎
　風はどっこどっこ又三郎」
　すると又三郎はまるであわてて、何かに足をひっぱられるように淵からとびあがって一目散にみんなのところに走ってきてがたがたふるえながら
「いま叫んだのはおまえらだちかい。」とききました。
「そでない、そでない。」みんな一しょに叫びました。ペ吉がまた一人出て来て、
「そでない。」と言いました。又三郎は、気味悪そうに川のほうを見ましたが色のあせた唇（くちびる）をいつものようにきっと嚙（か）んで
「何だい。」と言いましたが、からだはやはりがくがくふるっていました。
　そしてみんなは雨のはれ間を待ってめいめいのうちへ帰ったのです。

pitter-patter 「ざっこざっこ」、（雨の音が）パラパラ

howl-bellow 「どっこどっこ」

for dear life 「一目散に」、必死に

in unison 「一しょに」、声をそろえて

cleared up 「はれ間」が見える

12 September, Day Twelve

Howl and thunder ... howl roar HOWL!
Wind, blow off the fresh-green walnuts
Wind, blow off the sour quinces
Howl and thunder ... howl roar HOWL!
Howl and thunder ... howl roar HOWL!

Ichiro heard that very same song in a dream that he had heard Matasaburo sing. He bolted up, startled, to find the wind raging ferociously outside, the forest virtually roaring, and the whole house, from the paper sliding doors to the lantern box on the shelf, bathed in the pale blue light of the dawn sky. He quickly tied his belt, slipped into his clogs and stepped off the dirt floor outside and into the stable. When he opened a side door, the wind, reeking of rain, rushed in. A back door of the stable thudded down loudly and the horses were snorting up a storm.

Ichiro felt that the wind had made its way right into his heart, and he blew out a rush of breath and dashed outside, where it was already bright and the earth was soaked through. The chestnut trees all in a row in front of the house were strangely glowing pale blue, buffeted and tossed about, as if being washed and wrung out by the windy rain.

The earth was strewn with countless fresh green leaves and burrs that had been ripped from the blue-green chestnut trees, and the clouds, gray and foreboding in the light, were being carried at great speed northward. The forest in the distance was roaring like a raging sea. Ichiro stood fast, gazing up at the sky and listening to it all as his face was being battered by the cold rain, and it seemed as if his clothes were about to be torn right off him.

九月十二日、第十二日

「どっどど　どどうど　どどうど　どどう

青いくるみも、吹きとばせ

すっぱいかりんも吹きとばせ

どっどど　どどうど　どどうど　どどう

どっどど　どどうど　どどうど　どどう」

先頃又三郎から聞いたばかりのあの歌を一郎は夢の中でまたきいたのです。

びっくりして跳ね起きて見ると外ではほんとうにひどく風が吹いて林はまるで咆えるよう、あけがた近くの青ぐろい、うすあかりが障子や棚の上の提灯箱や家中一ぱいでした。一郎はすばやく帯をしてそして下駄をはいて土間を下り馬屋の前を通って潜りをあけましたら風がつめたい雨の粒と一緒にどうっと入って来ました。

馬屋のうしろの方で何か戸がばたっと倒れ馬はぶるるっと鼻を鳴らしました。一郎は風が胸の底まで滲み込んだように思ってはあと強く息を吐きました。そして外へかけだしました。外はもうよほど明るく土はぬれて居りました。家の前の栗の木の列は変に青く白く見えてそれがまるで風と雨とで今洗濯をするとでも言う様に烈しくもまれていました。青い葉も幾枚も吹き飛ばされ、ちぎられた青い栗のいがは黒い地面にたくさん落ちていました。空では雲がけわしい灰色に光りどんどんどんどん北の方へ吹きとばされていました。遠くの方の林はまるで海が荒れているようにごとんごとんと鳴ったりざっと聞えたりするのでした。一郎は顔いっぱいに冷たい雨の粒を投げつけられ風に着物をもって行かれそうになりながらだまってその音をききすましじっと空を見上げました。

raging　怒り狂う

roaring　「咆える」

paper sliding doors　「障子」

lantern box　「提灯箱」

dirt floor　「土間」

stable　「馬屋」

reeking of rain...　ぐっしょりになっている

thudded down　「倒れ」

in a row　一列の

glowing　光る、輝く

buffeted　何度も打たれて

tossed about　翻弄されて

wrung out　（水分を）絞り出される

strewn　ばら撒かれた

foreboding　悪い予感がする、虫の知らせがある

battered　「投げつけられ」、たたきのめされ

torn right off　はぎ取られ、もぎ取られ

He felt waves rippling through him and his heart started drumming and thumping as he watched and listened to the rushing wind groan and roar. The wind that had once been placid as it passed, lucid, over the hills and the fields below the sky had now moved in the dawn onto another plain as that sky coursed rapidly toward the northern edge of the Tuscarora Deep. Ichiro's face flushed feverishly, his breath caught in his throat and he felt as if he too was sailing with that wind through the sky. He rushed back into the house and, only when there, was he able to heave his chest and breathe out.

"Ah, this is a terrifying wind," said his grandfather, standing by the side door and peering into the sky. "With a wind like this, the tobacco plants and the chestnuts have had it."

Ichiro ran to the well, filled a bucket with water and went to the kitchen to mop and clean it up. Then he got out a metal basin and scrubbed his face, took some cold rice and miso from the cupboard and wolfed it down like there was no tomorrow.

"Ichiro, miso soup'll be ready in a jiffy so why don't you wait a minute," said his mother putting logs into the stove to make something for the horses. "What's the rush to get to school this morning?"

"Uh, Matasaburo might be in the air."

"What's Matasaburo, some bird or something?"

すると胸がさらさらと波をたてるように思いました。けれどもまたじっとその鳴って吠えてうなってかけて行く風をみていますと今度は胸がどかどかなってくるのでした。昨日まで丘や野原の空の底に澄みきってしんとしていた風が今朝夜あけ方俄かに一斉にこう動き出してどんどんどんどんタスカロラ海床の北のはじをめがけて行くことを考えますともう一郎は顔がほてり息もはあ、はあ、なって自分までが一緒に空を翔けて行くような気持ちになって胸を一ぱいはって息をふっと吹きました。

「ああひで風だ。今日はたばこも粟もすっかりやられる。」と一郎のおじいさんが潜りのところに立ってじっと空を見ています。一郎は急いで井戸からバケツに水を一ぱい汲んで台所をぐんぐん拭きました。それから金だらいを出して顔をぶるぶる洗うと戸棚から冷たいごはんと味噌をだしてまるで夢中でざくざく喰べました。

「一郎、いまお汁できるから少し待ってだらよ。何して今朝そったに早く学校へ行がないやないがべ。」

お母さんは馬にやる〔一字空白〕を煮るかまどに木を入れながらききました。

「うん。又三郎は飛んでったがも知れないもや。」

「又三郎って何だてや。鳥こだてが。」

rippling 「さらさらと波をたてる」、さざ波を立てる

thumping ドシンと大きな音を立てる

placid 「しんとして」、穏やかな、落ち着いた

lucid 「澄み切って」

Tuscarora Deep 「タスカロラ海床」。タスカロラ海淵、タスカロラ海溝とも呼ばれる。千島海溝東部の中央部にある、特に深い場所

have had it 「やらえる」、おしまいだ、もはやこれまでだ

in a jiffy 「いま」、すぐに、ただちに

"Uh, he's a boy named Matasaburo," said Ichiro, swallowing down the last mouthful of rice, washing up the bowl and, putting on a rainproof jacket that he took down from a hook in the kitchen, darting barefoot over to Kasuke's house with his clogs in his hands.

"I'll just eat a quick breakfast," said Kasuke, who had only then woken up.

Ichiro was waiting for him by the stable when Kasuke came out with a little straw rain cape over him. The two of them were soaked to the bone by the fierce windy rain by the time they reached school. They went in by the side entrance, but the classroom was deserted. Rain had made its way in through gaps in the windows and the floorboards were covered in a slippery film of water.

"Kasuke," said Ichiro, looking around, "let's sweep away the water together."

He got hold of a hemp-palm broom and started sweeping the water into cracks in the floor below the windows. They heard someone come in and saw the teacher, who, for some inexplicable reason, was wearing a single unlined garment and held a red fan in his hand.

「うん又三郎って言うやづよ。」一郎は急いでごはんをしまうと椀をこちこち洗って、それから台所の釘にかけてある油合羽を着て下駄はもってはだしで嘉助をさそいに行きました。嘉助はまだ起きたばかりで

「いまごはんをたべて行ぐがら。」と言いましたので一郎はしばらくうまやの前で待っていました。

まもなく嘉助は小さい簑を着て出てきました。

烈しい風と雨にぐしょぬれになりながら二人はやっと学校へ来ました。昇降口からはいって行きますと教室はまだしいんとしていましたがところどころの窓のすきまから雨が板にはいって板はまるでざぶざぶしていました。一郎はしばらく教室を見まわしてから

「嘉助、二人して水掃ぐべな。」と言ってしゅろ箒をもって来て水を窓の下の孔へはき寄せていました。

するともう誰か来たのかというように奥から先生が出てきましたがふしぎなことは先生があたり前の単衣をきて赤いうちわをもっているのです。

darting　飛んでいく、素早く動く

straw rain cape 「簑」

soaked to the bone 「ぐしょぬれになり」、びしょぬれになり

sweep away... 「水掃ぐ」、～を一掃する、～を押し流す

hemp-palm broom 「しゅろ箒」

cracks 「孔」、隙間

for some inexplicable reason 「ふしぎなことは」（inexplicable: 不可解な、説明できない）

unlined garment 「単衣」

"You boys are here early," he said. "Are you cleaning the classroom for us?"

"Good morning, teacher," said Ichiro.

"Good morning, teacher," said Kasuke, immediately adding, "Is Matasaburo coming to school today?"

"When you say Matasaburo, do you mean Takada Saburo?" he asked, after a short pause. "Well, he went with his father somewhere else yesterday. As it was a Sunday, he didn't have time to go around and tell everybody he was going."

"Sir, did he fly away?" asked Kasuke.

"No. His father received a telegram from his company headquarters to go. He plans, it seems, to return here but his son will be going to a school over there from now on. That's where his mother is, for one thing."

"Why was he called away by his company?" asked Ichiro.

"It seems that the vein of molybdenum here is not ready to be mined for some time."

"That can't be true," shrieked Kasuke. "It's because that boy was Matasaburo, the boy of the winds!"

Just then there was a clatter coming from the night-duty-man's room, and the teacher, holding his red fan, rushed into it.

Ichiro and Kasuke just stood there in silence for some time, staring into each other's eyes, as if seeking to read the other's thoughts.

The windows continued to rattle away, clouded over in raindrops sent by a wind that wasn't about to stop.

「たいへん早いですね。あなた方二人で教室の掃除をしているのですか。」先生がききました。

「先生お早うございます。」一郎が言いました。

「先生お早うございます。」嘉助も言いましたが、すぐ

「先生、又三郎今日来るのすか。」とききました。

先生はちょっと考えて

「又三郎って高田さんですか。ええ、高田さんは昨日お父さんといっしょにもう外へ行きました。日曜なのでみなさんにご挨拶するひまがなかったのです。」

「先生飛んで行ったのすか。」嘉助がききました。

「いいえ、お父さんが会社から電報で呼ばれたのです。お父さんはもいちどちょっとこっちへ戻られるそうですが高田さんはやっぱり向うの学校に入るのだそうです。向うにはお母さんも居られるのですから。」

「何して会社で呼ばったべす。」一郎がききました。

「ここのモリブデンの鉱脈は当分手をつけないことになった為なそうです。」

「そうだなぃな。やっぱりあいづは風の又三郎だったな。」

嘉助が高く叫びました。宿直室の方で何かごとごと鳴る音がしました。先生は赤いうちわをもって急いでそっちへ行きました。

二人はしばらくだまったまま相手がほんとうにどう思っているか探るように顔を見合わせたまま立ちました。

風はまだやまず、窓がらすは雨つぶのために曇りながらまだがたがた鳴りました。

after a short pause
「ちょっと考えて」、一瞬の間を置いて

telegram 「電報」

headquarters 「会社」、本社

vein 「鉱脈」

mined 採鉱される

shrieked 「高く叫びました」、金切り声を上げた

clatter 「ごとごと鳴る音」、カタカタいう音

night-duty-man's room 「宿直室」

clouded over in raindrops 「雨つぶのために曇りながら」

雪渡り
Snow Crossing

イラスト：ルーシー・バルバース

🔊 **8-9**

8: *p.*116 / 120　Part One　Konzaburo the Little Fox
9: *p.*136　Part Two　Magic Lantern Party
　　　　　　 at the Fox Elementary School

Snow Crossing を読むまえに

狐に包まれた人間たち

ある冬の日、四郎とかん子の兄妹は、小狐の紺三郎と知り合って楽しい
ひとときを過ごした。12 歳以上は来場お断りという狐の小学校の幻燈
会に誘われて……

　宮沢賢治の物語は、動物と人間の関係やふれあいについて教えてくれる、とても興味深いものです。賢治は、あらゆる生命の尊厳について心から深く信じていました。賢治の信念は、どんなに小さく、取るに足らないように見えるものであっても、すべての生き物を敬うという仏教の精神に由来しており、賢治が生きた時代の人々よりも、21世紀に生きる私たちのほうがはるかに共感できるものです。宮沢賢治は、作家として思想家として、彼が生きた時代の100年先をいっていたのです。

　『雪渡り』は、賢治の多くの物語と同様に人間と動物が入り交じる寓話です。この点では、賢治は何世紀にもわたって多くの国に存在した作家たちと似ています。しかし、彼は動物と人間を描く西洋の作家とは一線を画しています。多くのユダヤ教徒やキリスト教徒にとって、人間は生命の最高の形を象徴するものです。動物には魂がなく、人間と交流はあっても、対等な関係であることはほとんどありません。動物は一般に、人間を怖がらせるか、人間の要求に応えるかのどちらかです。ディズニー映画で人気のある物語では、動物はしばしば擬人化されています。つまり、動物のように見えるものは動物の皮をかぶった人間であり、人間が自分たちについての物語を作り上げるために、動物たちをかわいく見せたり、残酷に見せたりしているのです。

　賢治にとって、多くの場合、動物は人間と同等か、それ以上の存在です。その知性、感情、機知には目を瞠るものがあります。熊は仲間同士で語り合い、時には献身と慈愛を示し、山猫、鳥、鼠、猫などはおしゃべりをしながら、知恵と諦めと悲しみを示す。それを人間に伝え、無知な人間を啓蒙することもあります。

　そして、『雪渡り』の狐は、賢治の描く動物の中でも最も啓発的な存在です。

賢治は、賢い子狐の紺三郎と、人間の兄妹、四郎とかん子の出会いを、美しく抒情的な冒頭で演出します。大理石の板のような雪面、青い石板のような空、百合の香りのする太陽、ザラメのような霜で飾られた木々が登場します。なんと美しいのでしょうか！ 空、光、石のメタファーは、どんな出会いも人生を変えるきっかけになるかもしれないユニークな世界の縮図を作り出しています。

　さらに、「堅雪かんこ、しみ雪しんこ」という彼独自の歌のようなオノマトペが加わって、光と音による冒頭のイメージができあがり、空のメタファーを地球上の具体的なものに変えています。これは、冬の東北の風景を、子どもたち、それも小さな子どもたちの目を通して見たものであることに疑いの余地はないでしょう。子狐の紺三郎は、四郎とかん子の兄や12歳以上の人は幻燈会に参加できないことを、ふたりにちゃんと伝えています。

　四郎とかん子は、狐たちから、立派で道徳的な人間であること、酔ったり動物に残酷なことをしないこと、嘘をついたり人をうらやんだりしないことを教えられます。四郎とかん子は、狐と一緒に過ごすうちに、動物、それも残念ながら動物界ではどちらかと言うと評判のあんまり良くない狐を信頼することを学びます。

　四郎は紺三郎に「そいじゃきつねが人をだますなんて偽かしら」と聞きます。紺三郎は、次のようにあからさまに答えます。「偽ですとも。けだし最もひどい偽です。だまされたという人は大抵お酒に酔ったり、臆病でくるくるしたりした人です」。

　賢治は、酒を人の人生を破壊するものと見ていて、詩の中で、特に「政治家」と「住居」という詩の中で、酔っ払いを否定的に書いています。「政治家」では、政治家を「ひとさわぎおこして／いっぱい呑みたいやつら

ばかりだ」と揶揄しています。「住居」では、「ひるもはだしで酒を呑み／眼をうるませたとしよりたち」と、午後の太陽の下で酒を飲む姿を描いています。

　賢治が描く素敵な世界は、多くのオノマトペを伴う日本語で作られています。この物語を私が英語に訳したときに使った擬声語や擬態語や擬情語をいくつか紹介します。

　glittering、glistened（英語でglで始まる単語は光の現象に関係するものが多い）、squeak、creak、yelp、chuckle、puffy、fluffy、tap、yap、peep、blinking、thump。

　宮沢賢治の著作には、しばしば物語がクロスオーバーすることがありますが、『雪渡り』にもあの風の又三郎という少年が、ふーっと舞い込んでくるのが嬉しい。そして、四郎とかん子のポケットをドングリや栗や青びかりの石などでいっぱいにした後、狐の生徒たちも「風のように」立ち去って行きます。

　1921年12月と翌年1月に上下に分けて、母イチが所属していた愛国婦人会の機関誌「愛国婦人」に連載された『雪渡り』は、彼の作品の中で唯一、生前に原稿料が支払われた物語です。原稿料は5円でした。5円と言えば、当時、卵を5ダースほど買うことができる金額でした。

　しかし、賢治がお金に不自由していなかったのは事実です。岩手県内でも当時有数の資産家の出身であり、父親は長男の独断的な宗教観に反対しながらも、必要な時にはたいていの場合、彼を援助してくれました。このように、他人の窮状を救うために自己犠牲的に行動するのは、物質的に恵まれていることへの罪悪感を和らげるためという見方もできるでしょう。

Part One   Konzaburo the Little Fox

The snow was frozen stiff, even more solid than marble, and, to all appearances, the sky was a cold smooth blue sheet of stone.

Packed Snow, Cold Snow, Crunch and ... Slip!

The sun burned a pure white, releasing the fragrance of lily all about, glittering the snow below. As for the trees, they were dazzling, decked in a frost of what looked like icing sugar.

Packed Snow, Cold Snow, Crunch and ... Slip!

Shiro and Kanko went kicking and gliding into the fields in their little straw boots. Who could imagine a more fun day than this? They could go as far as they chose, over the meadows blanketed in pampas grass and through the millet fields which they couldn't always cross.

The plain was like a single sheet. And it glittered and glistened like so many tiny little mirrors.

Packed Snow, Cold Snow, Crunch and ... Slip!

The two children approached the forest. The body of a huge oak tree was bending from the weight of icicles embedded in it, hanging down splendorous and transparent. The two of them cried out at the top of their lungs, facing the forest.

Packed Snow, Cold Snow, Crunch and ... Slip! The little fox, he wants a bride, he does, he does!

雪渡り　その一（小狐の紺三郎）

　雪がすっかり凍って大理石よりも堅くなり、空も冷たい滑らかな青い石の板で出来ているらしいのです。

　「堅雪かんこ、しみ雪しんこ。」

　お日様がまっ白に燃えて百合の匂を撒きちらしまた雪をぎらぎら照らしました。

　木なんかみんなザラメを掛けたように霜でぴかぴかしています。

　「堅雪かんこ、凍み雪しんこ。」

　四郎とかん子とは小さな雪沓をはいてキックキックキック、野原に出ました。

　こんな面白い日が、またとあるでしょうか。いつもは歩けない黍の畑の中でも、すすきで一杯だった野原の上でも、すきな方へどこ迄でも行けるのです。平らなことはまるで一枚の板です。そしてそれが沢山の小さな小さな鏡のようにキラキラキラキラ光るのです。

　「堅雪かんこ、凍み雪しんこ。」

　二人は森の近くまで来ました。大きな柏の木は枝も埋まるくらい立派な透きとおった氷柱を下げて重そうに身体を曲げて居りました。

　「堅雪かんこ、凍み雪しんこ。狐の子ぁ、嫁ぃほしい、ほしい。」と二人は森へ向いて高く叫びました。

marble 「大理石」

to all appearances 「〜らしいのです」、どう見ても、明らかに

crunch 「かんこ」、ザクザク（雪を踏む音）

decked in a frost 「霜で」、霜に飾られて

icing sugar 「ザラメ」

straw boots 「雪沓」、わら製の深いくつ

pampas grass 「すすき」

millet fields 「黍の畑」

icicles 「氷柱」

cried out at the top of their lungs 「高く叫びました」、声を限りに叫んだ

For a time it was as quiet as a whisper, and when the two of them held their breath to cry out once more, the little white fox came out of the forest, padding over the creaking snow, saying …

Cold Snow, Slippery-slippery, Packed Snow, Squeak and Creak!

Shiro, slightly taken aback, shielded Kanko behind him, stood his ground and cried out …

Yelpy Fox, Icy Fox, if you want a bride, you'll have one too!

At that, the fox—though just a little slip of a fox—tweaked his taut silver needle-like whiskers and said …

Slippery Shiro, Crunchy Kanko, as for me I need no bride!

Shiro laughed and said …

Yelpy Fox, Little Fox, if you don't need a bride then have some rice cakes instead!

At that the little fox, shaking his head twice and thrice, merrily said …

Slippery Shiro, Crunchy Kanko, want my millet dumplings instead?

Kanko, hiding behind Shiro's back, was so tickled by this that she softly sang …

Yelpy Fox, Little Fox, your dumplings are made of rabbit poo!

しばらくしいんとしましたので二人はも一度叫ぼうとして息をのみこんだとき森の中から

「凍み雪しんしん、堅雪かんかん。」と言いながら、キシリキシリ雪をふんで白い狐の子が出て来ました。

四郎は少しぎょっとしてかん子をうしろにかばって、しっかり足をふんばって叫びました。

「狐こんこん白狐、お嫁ほしけりゃ、とってやろよ。」

すると狐がまだまるで小さいくせに銀の針のようなおひげをピンと一つひねって言いました。

「四郎はしんこ、かん子はかんこ、おらはお嫁はいらないよ。」

四郎が笑って言いました。

「狐こんこん、狐の子、お嫁がいらなきゃ餅やろか。」

すると狐の子も頭を二つ三つ振って面白そうに言いました。

「四郎はしんこ、かん子はかんこ、黍の団子をおれやろか。」

かん子もあんまり面白いので四郎のうしろにかくれたままそっと歌いました。

「狐こんこん狐の子、狐の団子は兎のくそ。」

held their breath 「息をのみこんだ」、息を止めた

padding over the creaking snow 「キシリキシリ雪をふんで」

taken aback 「ぎょっとして」

shielded Kanko behind 「かん子をうしろにかばって」

Yelpy 「こんこん」、（キツネが）コンコンと鳴く

though just a little slip of a fox 「まだまるで小さいくせに」、ほんの小狐なのに

rice cakes 「餅」

millet dumplings 「黍の団子」

was so tickled 「あんまり面白いので」

rabbit poo 「兎のくそ」

At that Konzaburo the Little Fox chuckled and said …

Oh no, that's absolutely wrong. Would fine upstanding humans like you ever consume things like brown rabbit dumplings? Up till now we have been falsely accused, I swear, of pulling the wool over the eyes of humans.

Shiro, surprised, asked the fox …

You mean, it's a lie about foxes outfoxing people?

Konzaburo answered earnestly …

Indubitably. Arguably the most unfair lie that ever was. The people who claim to be outfoxed by us are usually drunk or so chicken-hearted that they've gone bananas. You wouldn't believe it. Take Jinbei. Little while ago, on a moonlit night, he sat himself down in front of our house and sang traditional joruri ballads till late at night. Brought us all out for a look, it did.

Shiro cried out …

Jinbei wouldn't be singing traditional joruri ballads. It must have been traditional naniwabushi ballads!

Konzaburo seemed to agree with this …

すると小狐紺三郎が笑って言いました。

「いいえ、決してそんなことはありません。あなた方のような立派なお方が兎の茶色の団子なんか召しあがるもんですか。私らは全体いままで人をだますなんてあんまりむじつの罪をきせられていたのです。」

四郎がおどろいて尋ねました。

「そいじゃきつねが人をだますなんて偽かしら。」

紺三郎が熱心に言いました。

「偽ですとも。けだし最もひどい偽です。だまされたという人は大抵お酒に酔ったり、臆病でくるくるしたりした人です。面白いですよ。甚兵衛さんがこの前、月夜の晩私たちのお家の前に坐って一晩じょうるりをやりましたよ。私らはみんな出て見たのです。」

四郎が叫びました。

「甚兵衛さんならじょうるりじゃないや。きっと浪花ぶしだぜ。」

子狐紺三郎はなるほどという顔をして、

been falsely accused
「むじつの罪をきせられて」

pulling the wool over
the eyes 「だます」

outfoxing... 「〜をだます」、〜より一枚上手である、〜を出し抜く

indubitably 「偽ですとも」、間違いなく

Arguably 「けだし」、おそらく、間違いなく

chicken-hearted 「臆病で」

gone bananas 「くるくるした」、頭がおかしくなった

Yeah, you might be right. Anyway, have yourselves some dumplings. These dumplings of mine are the result of my diligently preparing the land, sowing the seeds, weeding the weeds, reaping, thrashing, making the flour, kneading the dough, steaming and sugaring them. How about it? Would you like a plateful?

Shiro laughed ...

My dear Konzaburo. We have only just eaten rice cakes now and are not in the least bit hungry. We'll take a rain check on these, if we may.

Konzaburo the Little Fox was pleased. He waved his short arms and said ...

If you wish. In any case, you can have some at the Magic Lantern Party. You wouldn't miss the Magic Lantern Party, would you? We'll meet on the evening of the next moonlit night when the snow freezes over. We start at eight, and I'll give you your admission tickets now. How many would you like?

Well, we'll take five then.

Five? That's two for you two, but who are the other three for?

Our elder brothers.

Are they eleven or under?

No, the youngest is in year four, and four plus eight makes twelve.

「ええ、そうかもしれません。とにかくお団子をおあがりなさい。私のさしあげるのは、ちゃんと私が畑を作って播いて草をとって刈って叩いて粉にして練ってむしてお砂糖をかけたのです。いかがですか。一皿さしあげましょう。」

と言いました。

と四郎が笑って、

「紺三郎さん、僕らは丁度いまね、お餅をたべて来たんだからおなかが減らないんだよ。この次におよばれしようか。」

子狐の紺三郎が嬉しがってみじかい腕をばたばたして言いました。

「そうですか。そんなら今度幻燈会のときさしあげましょう。幻燈会にはきっといらっしゃい。この次の雪の凍った月夜の晩です。八時からはじめますから、入場券をあげて置きましょう。何枚あげましょうか。」

「そんなら五枚おくれ。」と四郎が言いました。

「五枚ですか。あなた方が二枚にあとの三枚はどなたですか。」と紺三郎が言いました。

「兄さんたちだ。」と四郎が答えますと、

「兄さんたちは十一歳以下ですか。」と紺三郎がまた尋ねました。

「いや小兄さんは四年生だからね、八つの四つで十二歳。」と四郎が言いました。

a plateful 「一皿」、皿
1杯分

take a rain check 「この次におよばれしよう」、
またの機会にする

If you wish 「そうですか」、お好きなように、そうしたいのなら

Magic Lantern Party
「幻燈会」

admission tickets
「入場券」

At that, Konzaburo tweaked his whiskers like before, adding with a serious air ...

In that event, I regret to inform you that your elder brothers may not attend. Just you come. I'll set aside reserve seats for you. You'll have the time of your life.

The first slide takes up "Thou Shalt Not Drink" and it shows Taemon and Seisaku from your village who, having drunk themselves blue in the face, are just about to eat these funny buns and buckwheat noodles in the field. I'm in the photograph too.

The second one is entitled "Thou Shalt Be Wary Of Traps" and it depicts one of our number, Konbei, caught in a trap in a field. It's a picture. It's not a photograph.

The third is called "Thou Shalt Not Make Light Of Fire" and it shows a scene of one of our number, Konsuke, scorching his tail at your house. We'll be expecting you.

Most pleased, the two children nodded. The fox turned up the corner of his mouth as if highly amused himself, began to kick and tap, kick and tap his feet, then shook his tail and head in thought, finally appeared to have hit upon an idea and sang out in rhythm, waving both paws in the air ...

Cold Snow, Packed Snow, Slip and Crunch

The Buns in the Field are Puffy Puff Puff

するど紺三郎は尤もらしくまたおひげを一つひねって言いました。

「それでは残念ですが兄さんたちはお断わりです。あなた方だけいらっしゃい。特別席をとって置きますから、面白いんですよ。幻燈は第一が『お酒をのむべからず。』これはあなたの村の太右衛門さんと、清作さんがお酒をのんでとうとう目がくらんで野原にあるへんてこなおまんじゅうや、おそばを喰べようとした所です。私も写真の中にうつっています。第二が『わなに注意せよ。』これは私共のこん兵衛が野原でわなにかかったのを画いたのです。絵です。写真ではありません。第三が『火を軽べつすべからず。』これは私共のこん助があなたのお家へ行って尻尾を焼いた景色です。ぜひおいで下さい。」

二人は悦んでうなずきました。

狐は可笑しそうに口を曲げて、キックキックトントンキックキックトントンと足ぶみをはじめてしっぽと頭を振ってしばらく考えていましたがやっと思いついたらしく、両手を振って調子をとりながら歌いはじめました。

「凍み雪しんこ、堅雪かんこ、
　　　野原のまんじゅうはポッポッポ。

I'll set aside reserve seats 「特別席をとって置きます」

You'll have the time of your life 「面白いんですよ」

blue in the face 「目がくらんで」、顔が青くなるまで、いつまでも

buckwheat noodles 「おそば」

entitled ～という演題の

Thou Shalt Be Wary Of Traps 「わなに注意せよ」(Thou Shalt...: You Should...)

depicts 「画いたのです」

Thou Shalt Not Make Light Of Fire 「火を軽べつすべからず」

hit upon an idea 「思いついた」、よい考えを思いついた

Tipsy and Tottering is Good Ol' Taemon

Last year He Ate a Good Thirty-Eight Buns!

Cold Snow, Packed Snow, Slip and Crunch

The Noodles in the Field are Fluffy Fluff Fluff

Tipsy and Tottering is Good Ol' Seisaku

Last Year He Ate Thirteen Bowls Full!

Both Shiro and Kanko were carried away by the song, dancing in concert with the fox.

Kick kick tap tap ... kick kick tap tap ... kick kick kick kick ... tap tap tap!

Shiro sang out ...

Yelpy Fox, Little Fox, just last year Konbei the fox stuck his foot in a trap. Yelp yelp thump thump ... yelp yelp yelp!

Kanko sang out ...

Yelpy Fox, Little Fox, just last year Konsuke the fox picked a fish off the fire, burning his behind. Yap yap yap!

Kick tap tap... kick kick tap tap ... kick kick kick kick ... tap tap tap!

酔ってひょろひょろ太右衛門が、

　去年、三十八、たべた。

凍み雪しんこ、堅雪かんこ、

　野原のおそばはホッホッホ。

酔ってひょろひょろ清作が、

　去年十三ばいたべた。」

　四郎もかん子もすっかり釣り込まれてもう狐と一緒に踊っています。

　キック、キック、トントン。キック、キック、トントン。キック、キック、キック、キック、トントントン。

　四郎が歌いました。

　「狐こんこん狐の子、去年狐のこん兵衛が、ひだりの足をわなに入れ、こんこんばたばたこんこんこん。」

　かん子が歌いました。

　「狐こんこん狐の子、去年狐のこん助が、焼いた魚を取ろとしておしりに火がつききゃんきゃんきゃん。」

　キック、キック、トントン。キック、キック、トントン。キック、キック、キック、キックトントントン。

The three of them danced their way, step by step, into the woods.

The wind stirred the new red magnolia leaves, fashioned of sealing wax, causing them to flash in spurts, the indigo shadows of the trees spread their huge net onto the snow in the woods, and it looked as if silver lilies were blooming where the rays of the sun struck the ground.

At that, Konzaburo the Little Fox said ...

Should we ask the fawn to come here too? The little deer's so good at the flute.

Shiro and Kanko clapped their hands in delight, and the three of them cried out in unison ...

Packed Snow, Cold Snow, Crunch and Slip. The little deer, he wants a bride, he does, he does!

Then they heard a fine thin voice coming from the distance ...

The north wind goes peep, it's Saburo of the Wind. The west wind goes roar, it's Matasaburo again.

Konzaburo the Little Fox pouted his lips mockingly, saying ...

That's the fawn. He's much too timid to ever come over to us. But why don't we call to him once more?

The three of them cried out again ...

そして三人は踊りながらだんだん林の中にはいって行きました。赤い封蠟細工のほおの木の芽が、風に吹かれてピッカリピッカリと光り、林の中の雪には藍色の木の影がいちめん網になって落ちて日光のあたる所には銀の百合が咲いたように見えました。

すると子狐紺三郎が言いました。

「鹿の子もよびましょうか。鹿の子はそりゃ笛がうまいんですよ。」

四郎とかん子とは手を叩いてよろこびました。そこで三人は一緒に叫びました。

「堅雪かんこ、凍み雪しんこ、鹿の子ぁ嫁ぃほしいほしい。」

すると向うで、

「北風ぴいぴい風三郎、西風どうどう又三郎」と細いいい声がしました。

狐の子の紺三郎がいかにもばかにしたように、口を尖らして言いました。

「あれは鹿の子です。あいつは臆病ですからとてもこっちへ来そうにありません。けれどもう一遍叫んでみましょうか。」

そこで三人はまた叫びました。

red magnolia leaves 「赤い〜ほおの木の芽」、赤いホオノキの葉芽

fashioned of sealing wax 「封蝋細工の」

flash in spurts 「ピッカリピッカリと光り」、一気に光り

fawn 「鹿の子」

the north wind goes peep 「北風ぴいぴい」、北風がピーピー吹く

pouted his lips mockingly 「いかにもばかにしたように、口を尖らして」

Packed Snow, Cold Snow, Crunch and Slip. The little deer, he wants a bride, he does, he does!

From far far away they heard what sounded like the wind or a flute or, perhaps, a fawn's song ...

The north wind goes peep, too cold to sleep

The west wind goes roar, knocks on my door

The fox tweaked his whiskers again and said ...

We can't wait till the snow gets all soft, so go on home now. Come again, won't you, when the snow freezes over on a moonlit night. We'll do the magic lantern I told you about.

Shiro and Kanko sang out ...

Packed Snow, Cold Snow, Crunch and Slip

They crossed over the silvery snow toward home.

Packed Snow, Cold Snow, Crunch and Slip!

「堅雪かんこ、凍み雪しんこ、しかの子ぁ嫁ほしい、ほしい。」

　すると今度はずうっと遠くで風の音か笛の声か、または鹿の子の歌かこんなように聞えました。

「北風ぴいぴい、かんこかんこ
　　　　西風どうどう、どっこどっこ。」

　狐がまたひげをひねって言いました。

「雪が柔らかになるといけませんからもうお帰りなさい。今度月夜に雪が凍ったらきっとおいで下さい。さっきの幻燈をやりますから。」

　そこで四郎とかん子とは

「堅雪かんこ、凍み雪しんこ。」と歌いながら銀の雪を渡っておうちへ帰りました。

「堅雪かんこ、凍み雪しんこ。」

tweaked his whiskers 「ひげをひねって」

Part Two   Magic Lantern Party at the Fox Elementary School

An enormous pale full moon rose slowly over Ice Mountain. The snow gleamed blue in its light and, once again today, froze solid like a slab of white marble.

Shiro recalled his promise to Konzaburo the Little Fox and said softly to his little sister, Kanko ...

Tonight's the foxes' Magic Lantern Party. Should we go to it?

At that, Kanko jumped up and cried out ...

Yes, let's. We should. Yelpy Fox, Little Fox, Yelpy Konzaburo the Fox!

Then Jiro, the second oldest brother, said ...

Are you two going to visit the fox? I want to go too.

Shiro shrugged his shoulders at a loss for what to do, saying ...

Oh, Jiro. But the foxes' Magic Lantern Party is only for children up to eleven. That's what it says on the ticket.

Jiro replied ...

What ticket? Lemme see. Uh-huh. "We beg to inform you that save for the immediate family of the school's pupils no one twelve or over will be permitted entrance." Boy, these foxes sure are professional. I can't go, I guess. Can't be helped. But if you're going, take some rice cakes for them with you. Here, these mirror-shaped ones are just the thing.

雪渡り　その二（狐小学校の幻燈会）

　青白い大きな十五夜のお月様がしずかに氷の上山から登りました。

　雪はチカチカ青く光り、そして今日も寒水石のように堅く凍りました。

　四郎は狐の紺三郎との約束を思い出して妹のかん子にそっと言いました。

「今夜狐の幻燈会なんだね。行こうか。」

　するとかん子は、

「行きましょう。行きましょう。狐こんこん狐の子、こんこん狐の紺三郎。」とはねあがって高く叫んでしまいました。

　すると二番目の兄さんの二郎が

「お前たちは狐のとこへ遊びに行くのかい。僕も行きたいな。」と言いました。

　四郎は困ってしまって肩をすくめて言いました。

「大兄さん。だって、狐の幻燈会は十一歳までですよ、入場券に書いてあるんだもの。」

　二郎が言いました。

「どれ、ちょっとお見せ、ははあ、学校生徒の父兄にあらずして十二歳以上の来賓は入場をお断わり申し候、狐なんて仲々うまくやってるね。僕はいけないんだね。仕方ないや。お前たち行くんならお餅を持って行っておやりよ。そら、この鏡餅がいいだろう。」

an enormous pale full moon 「青白い大きな十五夜のお月様」

slab of white marble 「寒水石」、白い大理石の厚板

at a loss 「困ってしまって」、途方に暮れて

Lemme see 「ちょっとお見せ」、見せてくれ、どれどれ（Lemme see: Let me see）

immediate family of the school's pupils 「学校生徒の父兄」、生徒たちの近親者

mirror-shaped ones 「鏡餅」、鏡の形をした餅

Shiro and Kanko put on their little straw boots and went out carrying the rice cakes. Ichiro, the eldest brother, Jiro the second and Saburo the third stood side by side in the doorway.

Bye-bye. If you meet up with an adult fox, be sure to shut your eyes right away. Now we'll sing for you. Packed Snow, Cold Snow, Crunch and Slip. The little fox he wants a bride, he does, he does!

And the moon rose high in the sky and the forest was shrouded in pale smoke. The two children arrived at the entrance to the forest. A little white baby fox, with an acorn badge pinned to his chest, was standing there ...

Good evening. Good morning. Do you have a ticket?

We do.

The two of them showed their tickets.

Well then, this way please.

The baby fox leaned forward formally and, winking and blinking all the while, indicated a point inside the forest with his paw. The moonlight shone down as if hurled on an angle into the forest like any number of bolts of blue. The children came to a clearing in the forest. There they saw lots of pupils from Fox Elementary School already gathered, throwing chestnut shells at each other and practicing sumo. The funniest thing of all was the teeny-weeny little fox, no bigger than a mouse, riding piggyback on the large young fox while trying to reach for the stars.

四郎とかん子はそこで小さな雪沓をはいてお餅をかつ
いで外に出ました。

　兄弟の一郎二郎三郎は戸口に並んで立って、

　「行っておいで。大人の狐にあったら急いで目をつぶ
るんだよ。そら僕ら囃してやろうか。堅雪かんこ、凍み
雪しんこ、狐の子ぁ嫁ぃほしいほしい。」と叫びました。

　お月様は空に高く登り森は青白いけむりに包まれてい
ます。二人はもうその森の入口に来ました。

　すると胸にどんぐりのきしょうをつけた白い小さな狐
の子が立って居て言いました。

　「今晩は。お早うございます。入場券はお持ちですか。」

　「持っています。」二人はそれを出しました。

　「さあ、どうぞあちらへ。」狐の子が尤もらしくからだ
を曲げて眼をパチパチしながら林の奥を手で教えまし
た。

　林の中には月の光が青い棒を何本も斜めに投げ込んだ
ように射して居りました。その中のあき地に二人は来ま
した。

　見るともう狐の学校生徒が沢山集って栗の皮をぶっつ
け合ったりすもうをとったり殊におかしいのは小さな小
さな鼠位の狐の子が大きな子供の狐の肩車に乗ってお
星様を取ろうとしているのです。

If you meet up with...
「〜にあったら」、偶然〜に
出会ったら

acorn badge 「どんぐ
りのきしょう」

winking and blinking
「眼をパチパチしながら」

as if hurled on an
angle 「斜めに投げ込ん
だように」

bolts of blue 「青い
棒」、青色の稲妻

chestnut　栗

teeny-weeny little
fox 「小さな小さな〜狐
の子」

riding piggyback
on... 「〜の肩車に乗っ
て」

A white sheet was hanging from the branch of a tree in front of them. Out of the blue they heard a voice behind them ...

Good evening. So nice of you to come. It was a pleasure seeing you the other day.

Shiro and Kanko turned about in surprise to see Konzaburo before them. Konzaburo, sporting an elegant swallow-tail coat and a narcissus on his chest, was busily wiping his pointy mouth with a snow-white handkerchief.

Shiro, bowing slightly, said ...

The pleasure's all ours. And also, thank you for tonight. These rice cakes are for all of you to eat.

All of the pupils at Fox Elementary School were staring at them. Konzaburo puffed his chest fully out and proudly received the rice cakes.

I cannot thank you enough for this gift. Please make yourselves every bit at home. The magic lantern show will begin in two shakes of a lamb's tail. Now, if you will excuse me.

Konzaburo left them, taking the rice cakes with him. The pupils at Fox Elementary School cried out in unison ...

Packed Snow, Cold Snow, Crunch and Slip. Hard rice cakes will crack your snout ... white rice cakes will slither about!

みんなの前の木の枝に白い一枚の敷布がさがっていました。

　不意にうしろで

　「今晩は、よくおいででした。先日は失礼いたしました。」という声がしますので四郎とかん子とはびっくりして振り向いて見ると紺三郎です。

　紺三郎なんかまるで立派な燕尾服を着て水仙の花を胸につけてまっ白なはんけちでしきりにその尖ったお口を拭いているのです。

　四郎はちょっとお辞儀をして言いました。

　「この間は失敬。それから今晩はありがとう。このお餅をみなさんであがって下さい。」

　狐の学校生徒はみんなこっちを見ています。

　紺三郎は胸を一杯に張ってすまして餅を受けとりました。

　「これはどうもおみやげを戴いて済みません。どうかごゆるりとなすって下さい。もうすぐ幻燈もはじまります。私はちょっと失礼いたします。」

　紺三郎はお餅を持って向うへ行きました。

　狐の学校生徒は声をそろえて叫びました。

　「堅雪かんこ、凍み雪しんこ、硬いお餅はかったらこ、白いお餅はべったらこ。」

swallow-tail coat 「燕尾服」

narcissus 「水仙の花」

pointy mouth 「尖ったお口」

puffed his chest fully out 「胸を一杯に張って」

in two shakes of a lamb's tail 「もうすぐ」。子羊が尾を2振りする時間が極めて短いと感じられることから、あっという間にという意味

slither about 「べったらこ」、一面に広がる、這う。snout と韻を踏んでいる

A large sign appeared next to the curtain.

> RECEIVED: ONE PILE OF RICE CAKES FROM MASTER
> SHIRO, HUMAN BEING AND MISS KANKO, ALSO HUMAN
> BEING

The fox pupils clapped their paws in glee. At that moment, a whistle whistled. Konzaburo cleared his throat with two "ahems" as he appeared to one side of the curtain, bowing politely.

This quietened everyone down.

We have superb weather tonight. The moon may as well be a plate made of pearls. The stars appear to be dew on the meadow fixed in permanent twinkling. Now it's time for the Magic Lantern Party. I ask all of you to open your eyes as wide as you can and refrain from blinking and sneezing. Furthermore, I request that you all remain silent this evening in deference to our two honored guests. There will be no tossing of chestnut shells in their direction. This concludes my opening remarks.

They all clapped their paws in glee. Then Shiro said quietly to Kanko ...

Konzaburo really knows his stuff, doesn't he.

The whistle whistled again, and THOU SHALT NOT DRINK was projected onto the screen in large type. Then that was replaced with a photograph. It depicted a drunk old human male with his hands around some funny round object. They all stamped their feet and sang out ...

幕の横に、

「寄贈、お餅餅沢山、人の四郎氏、人のかん子氏」と大きな札が出ました。狐の生徒は悦んで手をパチパチ叩きました。

その時ピーと笛が鳴りました。

紺三郎がエヘンエヘンとせきばらいをしながら幕の横から出て来て丁寧にお辞儀をしました。みんなはしんとなりました。

「今夜は美しい天気です。お月様はまるで真珠のお皿です。お星さまは野原の露がキラキラ固まったようです。さて只今から幻燈会をやります。みなさんは瞬やくしゃみをしないで目をまんまろに開いて見ていて下さい。

それから今夜は大切な二人のお客さまがありますからどなたも静かにしないといけません。決してそっちの方へ栗の皮を投げたりしてはなりません。開会の辞です。」

みんな悦んでパチパチ手を叩きました。そして四郎がかん子にそっと言いました。

「紺三郎さんはうまいんだね。」

笛がピーと鳴りました。

『お酒をのむべからず』大きな字が幕にうつりました。そしてそれが消えて写真がうつりました。一人のお酒に酔った人間のおじいさんが何かおかしな円いものをつかんでいる景色です。

みんなは足ぶみをして歌いました。

cleared his throat 「せきばらいをしながら」

ahems 「エヘンエヘン」

This quietened everyone down 「みんなはしんとなりました」

refrain from blinking and sneezing 「瞬やくしゃみをしないで」

in deference to our two honored guests 「大切な二人のお客さまがありますから」、2人の賓客に敬意を表して

opening remarks 「開会の辞」

Kick kick tap tap, kick kick tap tap

Cold Snow, Packed Snow, Slip and Crunch

The Buns in the Field are Puffy Puff Puff

Tipsy and Tottering is Good Ol' Taemon

Last Year He Ate a Good Thirty-Eight Buns!

Kick kick kick kick, tap tap tap!

The photograph disappeared. Shiro said softly to Kanko ...

That's Konzaburo's song.

Another photograph came on. A young drunk human was eating something with his head buried in a bowl-like object made of a magnolia leaf. Konzaburo was watching in the distance wearing a white hakama. They all stamped their feet and sang out ...

Kick kick tap tap, kick kick tap tap

Cold Snow, Packed Snow, Slip and Crunch

The Noodles in the Field are Fluffy Fluff Fluff

Tipsy and Tottering is Good Ol' Seisaku

Last Year He Ate Thirteen Bowls Full!

Kick kick kick kick, tap tap tap!

キックキックトントンキックキックトントン
　凍み雪しんこ、堅雪かんこ、
　　　　野原のまんじゅうはぽっぽっぽ
　酔ってひょろひょろ太右衛門が
　　　去年、三十八たべた。
キックキックキックキックトントントン
写真が消えました。四郎はそっとかん子に言いました。
「あの歌は紺三郎さんのだよ。」
　別に写真がうつりました。一人のお酒に酔った若い者がほおの木の葉でこしらえたお椀のようなものに顔をつっ込んで何か喰べています。紺三郎が白い袴をはいて向うで見ているけしきです。
　みんなは足踏みをして歌いました。
キックキックトントン、キックキック、トントン、
　凍み雪しんこ、堅雪かんこ、
　　　　野原のおそばはぽっぽっぽ、
　酔ってひょろひょろ清作が
　　　去年十三ばい喰べた。
キック、キック、キック、キック、トン、トン、トン。

The photograph went off and a short interval followed. An adorable little vixen came around with two plates of millet dumplings. Shiro was at a complete loss for what to do. This was because he had just seen Taemon and Seisaku eating something bad without realizing it. In addition, all the pupils at Fox Elementary School were turned toward them, whispering among themselves ...

Will they eat one? What do you think, will they eat one?

Kanko just held a plate in her hand, blushing bashfully from ear to ear. At that, Shiro made up his mind and said ...

It's all right. Let's eat them. Come on, eat up. I don't really think Konzaburo is pulling a fast one on us.

The two of them ate up all the millet dumplings. They tasted like heaven. The pupils at Fox Elementary School jumped for joy and danced about ...

Kick kick tap tap, kick kick tap tap

By day the sun beats down its light

By night the moon is blue and bright

Break their bones and let them die

No fox pupil would ever lie

写真が消えてちょっとやすみになりました。

可愛らしい狐の女の子が黍団子をのせたお皿を二つ持って来ました。

四郎はすっかり弱ってしまいました。なぜってたった今太右衛門と清作との悪いものを知らないで喰べたのを見ているのですから。

それに狐の学校生徒がみんなこっちを向いて「食うだろうか。ね。食うだろうか。」なんてひそひそ話し合っているのです。かん子ははずかしくてお皿を手に持ったまままっ赤になってしまいました。すると四郎が決心して言いました。

「ね、喰べよう。お喰べよ。僕は紺三郎さんが僕らを欺すなんて思わないよ。」そして二人は黍団子をみんな喰べました。そのおいしいことは頬っぺたも落ちそうです。狐の学校生徒はもうあんまり悦んでみんな踊りあがってしまいました。

キックキックトントン、キックキックトントン。

「ひるはカンカン日のひかり
よるはツンツン月あかり、
たとえからだを、さかれても
狐の生徒はうそ言うな。」

キック、キックトントン、キックキックトントン。

「ひるはカンカン日のひかり
よるはツンツン月あかり
たとえこごえて倒れても
狐の生徒はぬすまない。」

a short interval 「一寸やすみ」、短い幕間

was at a complete loss 「すっかり弱ってしまいました」、完全に途方に暮れた

blushing bashfully from ear to ear 「はずかしくて〜まっ赤になってしまいました」、恥ずかしそうに顔を（耳から耳まで）真っ赤にして

pulling a fast one on us 「僕らを欺すなんて」

tasted like heaven 「そのおいしいことは頬っぺたも落ちそう」、天国のような味がした、最高においしかった

the sun beats down 「カンカン日のひかり」、太陽が照りつける

Kick kick tap tap, kick kick tap tap

By day the sun beats down its light

By night the moon is blue and bright

Push them down in snow and hail

No fox pupil would ever steal

Kick kick tap tap, kick kick tap tap

By day the sun beats down its light

By night the moon is blue and bright

Tear them from their fathers and mothers

No fox pupil would envy others

Kick kick tap tap, kick kick tap tap

Shiro and Kanko wept for sheer joy. The whistle whistled and THOU SHALT NOT MAKE LIGHT OF TRAPS appeared on the sheet in large lettering before it was replaced by a picture. This one pictured Konbei the fox with his left foot caught in a trap.

キックキックトントン、キックキックトントン。

　「ひるはカンカン日のひかり

　よるはツンツン月あかり

　たとえからだがちぎれても

　狐の生徒はそねまない。」

キックキックトントン、キックキックトントン。

四郎もかん子もあんまり嬉しくて涙がこぼれました。

笛がピーとなりました。

『わなを軽べつすべからず』と大きな字がうつりそれ

が消えて絵がうつりました。狐のこん兵衛がわなに左足

をとられた景色です。

hail　霰

Tear them from their
fathers and mothers
「たとえからだがちぎれて
も」、彼らを両親から引き
離しても

THOU SHALT NOT
MAKE LIGHT OF
TRAPS　「わなを軽べつ
すべからず」（make light
of: 軽く見る、軽んじる）

Yelpy Fox, Little Fox, just last year Konbei the fox stuck his foot in a trap.

Yelp yelp thump thump, yelp yelp yelp!

That's what they all sang. Shiro said softly to Kanko ...

That's the song I made up.

The picture was replaced with the words THOU SHALT NOT MAKE LIGHT OF FIRE, then that disappeared and another picture came on. It showed Konsuke the fox getting his tail on fire by reaching for a grilled fish. All of the fox pupils cried out ...

Yelpy Fox, Little Fox, just last year Konsuke the fox picked a fish off the fire, burning his behind. Yap yap yap!

The whistle whistled, the curtain lit up and once again Konzaburo appeared and said ...

Well, everyone, that concludes tonight's magic lantern show. There is something that you all must truly take to heart tonight, and that is the fact that two children, who are human beings, both clever and not in the least drunk, have been kind enough to eat food made by foxes. I believe that in the future you, as adults, will neither tell lies nor be envious of others, and that the bad reputation we foxes have had up till now will be a thing of the past. This concludes my closing remarks.

「狐こんこん狐の子、去年狐のこん兵衛が
　左の足をわなに入れ、こんこんばたばた
　　　　　　　　　　こんこんこん。」

とみんなが歌いました。

四郎がそっとかん子に言いました。

「僕の作った歌だねい。」

絵が消えて『火を軽べつすべからず』という字があらわれました。それも消えて絵がうつりました。狐のこん助が焼いたお魚を取ろうとしてしっぽに火がついた所です。

狐の生徒がみな叫びました。

「狐こんこん狐の子。去年狐のこん助が
　焼いた魚を取ろとしておしりに火がつき
　　　　　　　　　　きゃんきゃんきゃん。」

笛がピーと鳴り幕は明るくなって紺三郎がまた出て来て言いました。

「みなさん。今晩の幻燈はこれでおしまいです。今夜みなさんは深く心に留めなければならないことがあります。それは狐のこしらえたものを賢いすこしも酔わない人間のお子さんが喰べて下すったという事です。そこでみなさんはこれからも、大人になってもうそをつかず人をそねまず私共狐の今迄の悪い評判をすっかり無くしてしまうだろうと思います。閉会の辞です。」

getting his tail on fire
「しっぽに火がついた」

grilled fish 「焼いた魚」

behind 「おしり」

curtain lit up 「幕は明るくなって」

take to heart 「深く心に留めなければ」、深く心に刻む

closing remarks 「閉会の辞」

The pupils were moved, down to the last fox, raising both paws and rushing to their feet. Their cheeks glittered in tears. Konzaburo came to the two children and bowed politely, saying ...

Well, this is goodbye. I am eternally grateful to you for tonight.

The two of them also bowed and went on their way toward home. The fox pupils caught up with them and filled all their pockets with acorns and chestnuts and phosphorescent stones.

Here, these are for you.

Here, please have these.

This is what they said before departing like the wind itself. Konzaburo watched with a smile on his lips.

The two children left the forest and started across the field. When they reached the very middle of that field of the palest snow, they caught sight of three dark shadows approaching them from a distance. The shadows belonged to their elder brothers who were coming for them.

狐の生徒はみんな感動して両手をあげたりワーッと立ちあがりました。そしてキラキラ涙をこぼしたのです。

　紺三郎が二人の前に来て、丁寧におじぎをして言いました。

　「それでは。さようなら。今夜のご恩は決して忘れません。」

　二人もおじぎをしてうちの方へ帰りました。狐の生徒たちが追いかけて来て二人のふところやかくしにどんぐりだの栗だの青びかりの石だのを入れて、

　「そら、あげますよ。」「そら、取って下さい。」なんて言って風の様に逃げ帰って行きます。

　紺三郎は笑って見ていました。

　二人は森を出て野原を行きました。

　その青白い雪の野原のまん中で三人の黒い影が向うから来るのを見ました。それは迎いに来た兄さん達でした。

raising both paws
「両手をあげたり」、前足を両方とも上げて

rushing to their feet
「ワーッと立ちあがりました」、急いで立ち上がって

caught up with... 「追いかけて来て」、追いついて

phosphorescent stones 「青びかりの石」、蓄光石。（phosphorescent：燐光を発する、青光りする）

よだかの星
The Nighthawk Star

イラスト：ルーシー・パルバース

The Nighthawk Star を読むまえに

ひかりはたもたれ、電燈は失われ

鷹からいじめられ、星たちから蔑まれ、常に冷たい扱いを受けるよだか。
しかし星になろうと決意したよだかは、ついに自力で天上を目指す。

🔊 10　　*p*.154 /158

よだかは賢治の物語における負け犬の典型です。

よだかは決して美しくはなく、威厳もありません。よだかは、賢治の世界の多くの生き物がそうであるように、他から自分が気に入られ、自分の存在価値が評価されることを望んでいます。しかし他の鳥たちや星たちに何度も肘鉄砲を食わせられるわけです。おまけに、泣き面に蜂というか、鷹は、よだかの名前の中に、「たか」という名前が入っているのがけしからんと、よだかに対して難癖をつけ、名前を変えて他の鳥たちに改名したことを披露するよう要求します。

「鳥のうちを一軒ずつまわって、お前が来たかどうかを聞いてあるく」と鷹は警告します。「一軒でも来なかったという家があったら、もう貴様もその時がおしまいだぞ」と。

よだかは明らかにいじめにあっていますが、この鷹の警告に従うしかありません。よだかはあちこちを飛び回りますが、そのとき、開いたくちばしに羽虫や甲虫が引っかかります。言うまでもなく、生きるためにはそういったものを飲み込んで食べなければなりません。しかし、よだかは喉に引っかかった甲虫のために涙を流すのです。いっそのこと、自分は食べるのをやめて餓死したほうがいいのではないか。そうしたら、もしかすると、天高くまで飛んでいき、星に仲間に入れてくれと頼むことができるかもしれないと。

しかし、星たちもよだかを蔑むばかりでした。大熊星は、「氷山の浮いている海」に飛び込むか、近くにそのような海がなければ「氷をうかべたコップの水の中」に飛び込むことで涼をとることを提案し、よだかを嘲笑します。またしても、賢治のキャラクターは他人からバカにされ、「でくの坊」と見なされています。

夜の生き物であるよだかは、自分も星になりたいと思っています。しかし、他の星々はそんな思いを抱くよだかをガミガミと怒鳴って叱っています。

「星になるには、それ相応の身分でなくちゃいかん」。相当な金が必要なのはいうまでもありません。

　ここで社会批評家の宮沢賢治は、世の中の厳しい現実を読者に知らせているのです。

　よだかは美しくも雄々しくもないかもしれませんが、力強い翼を持っています。彼は自力で星になるために高く飛ぼうと決意します。翼がしびれ、くちばしから血がにじみ出るほど（賢治自身や他の結核患者のことを暗示している）、これ以上ないというほどの努力が必要でしたが、よだかはついに、二度と地球に戻る必要がないほど高く天上まで飛ぶことに成功します。

　『よだかの星』は、1934年に初めて活字になって以来、賢治の最も人気のある物語のひとつです。理由は明らかです。この短い抒情的な散文詩は美しく書かれており、無私無欲の明確なメッセージを伝えているからです。よだかは星になりたいと願いますが、自分が有名になるためではありません。彼には二つの切迫した動機があるのです。

　第一に、星になることで、すべての生き物に永遠に光を与えることができるからです。これはまさに、『銀河鉄道の夜』のサソリが目指していることです。他者に奉仕するために自らの存在を消し去る必要があるのなら、それこそが進むべき道なのです。この信念は、賢治の熱心な仏教信仰からきています。

　ふたつ目の動機もまた、彼の信仰から引き出されたものです。星は決して落ちないほど高いところにあります。そこまで上れる生き物であれば、この世に戻る必要のない場所までたどり着くことができます。すなわち、究極の楽園です。生まれ変わりのサイクルから解き放たれる場所、カンパネルラが行った場所です。

　この物語に登場する鳥の正式な名前は「よたか」です。東北弁、（あ

るいは賢治が作った「東北弁風」）で「よだか」と言います。宮沢賢治の
著作には方言がよく出てくると言われています。しかし実際には、賢治
が方言を使うことはむしろ比較的稀で、彼の物語や詩の台詞はほとん
どすべて標準語で書かれています。賢治が作品に方言を使用した最たる例
としては、短編『鹿踊りのはじまり』と戯曲の『種山ヶ原』があります。

　beeline（一直線））＜本文p.166＞や dead as a dodo（完全に死んで）
＜p.162＞のように、訳文には多くの地口を入れました。beelineは、蜂
(bee)のまっすぐな飛び方を意味します。dodoは、絶滅された鳥の名前
です。dの音も繰り返されていて、語呂のいい決まり文句となっています。
また、What in heaven's name ＜p.172＞というフレーズも一種の語呂合
わせです。賢治には日本語の「空」をダジャレにした作品がいくつかあ
ります。「ほら」の変化形であるひらがなの「そら」を「見ろ！」という
意味でも使っています。

　よだかにちなんで名付けられた星は、公式には存在しません。しかし、
賢治が星座を熟知していたことは確かです。「よだか」という星の位置は、
デンマークの天文学者ティコ・ブラーエが1572年に発見した超新星の
位置を表しています。死の間際に爆発したこの星の残骸は、カシオペア
座の星雲として今日でも見ることができます。賢治はおそらく、これを
意識して、よだかを飛ばせたはずです。

　ジェイムズ・ジョイスが『ユリシーズ』の中でティコが発見した超新
星に言及していたことは、賢治は知らなかったのです。ティコがこの星
を発見したとき8歳だったウィリアム・シェイクスピアが『ハムレット』
の中で言及しているのは、おそらくこの星のことだったでしょうが、賢
治はこれも知りませんでした。しかし、最後の一行、「今でもまだ燃えて
います」の言葉はちゃんと、自然科学の事実に基づいています。これも「賢
治リアリズム」の shining example（輝く例）ではないでしょうか。

The nighthawk is truly an ugly bird. His face is blotchy in spots, as if splattered with miso, and his flat beak is split right up to his ears. He can barely totter six feet on those legs of his, and other birds get totally disgusted at the mere sight of his face.

For instance, the skylark isn't exactly what you would call a pretty bird, but it considers itself head and shoulders above the nighthawk. When it comes across the nighthawk in the evening, it clamps its eyelids shut and looks the other way, as if it will have nothing to do with him. The littler chatty birds just jump at the chance to say bad things to the nighthawk right under his beak.

"Humph. Here he comes again. Just look at that. He really gives us birds a bad name."

"Yeah, I mean, have you ever seen a mouth that big? He must be related to frogs or something."

That's the sort of thing they say. Oh, if the nighthawk was not a nighthawk but just a plain hawk instead, those shallow little birds would just shake and quiver at the mere sound of his name. They would go pale as ghosts, shrivel up into little balls and hide in the shade of some leafy tree.

But the fact of the matter is, the nighthawk is no brother to the hawk. He's not even related. He's really the big brother of that beautiful kingfisher and that jewel of a bird, the hummingbird. The hummingbird drinks nectar from flowers and the kingfisher eats fish, while the nighthawk lives off bird lice. And even the weakest birds aren't really afraid of the nighthawk, because his claws and beak are not in the least bit sharp.

nighthawk 「よだか」、
よたか。ヨタカ科の鳥。夕
刻から活動して、飛びなが
ら虫を捕まえて食べる

blotchy in spots 「と
ころどころ〜まだらで」、
ところどころ斑点のある
（blotchy: しみの多い）

flat beak 「くちばしは、
ひらたくて」、平たいくち
ばし

barely totter 「足は、
まるでよぼよぼで」、かろ
うじてよちよち歩く

head and shoulders
above... 「〜よりは、
ずっと上」、〜よりはるか
に優れている

right under his beak
「まっこうから」。right
under his nose の
nose を beak で言い換え
ている（right under his
nose: すぐ目の前で、はっ
きりと）

shrivel up into little
balls 「からだをちぢめ
て」、からだを縮こめて丸
くなる

the fact of the matter
is 「ところが」、実は、実
際には

kingfisher 「かわせみ」

hummingbird 「蜂すず
め」、ハチドリ

lives off bird lice 「羽
虫をとってたべる」、ハジ
ラミを食べて生きていく

　よだかは、実にみにくい鳥です。

　顔は、ところどころ、味噌をつけたようにまだらで、くちばしは、ひらたくて、耳までさけています。

　足は、まるでよぼよぼで、一間とも歩けません。

　ほかの鳥は、もう、よだかの顔を見ただけでも、いやになってしまうという工合でした。

　たとえば、ひばりも、あまり美しい鳥ではありませんが、よだかよりは、ずっと上だと思っていましたので、夕方など、よだかにあうと、さもさもいやそうに、しんねりと目をつぶりながら、首をそっ方へ向けるのでした。もっとちいさなおしゃべりの鳥などは、いつでもよだかのまっこうから悪口をしました。

　「ヘン。また出て来たね。まあ、あのざまをごらん。ほんとうに、鳥の仲間のつらよごしだよ。」

　「ね、まあ、あのくちのおおきいことさ。きっと、かえるの親類か何かなんだよ。」

　こんな調子です。おお、よだかでないただのたかならば、こんな生はんかのちいさい鳥は、もう名前を聞いただけでも、ぶるぶるふるえて、顔色を変えて、からだをちぢめて、木の葉のかげにでもかくれたでしょう。ところが夜だかは、ほんとうは鷹の兄弟でも親類でもありませんでした。かえって、よだかは、あの美しいかわせみや、鳥の中の宝石のような蜂すずめの兄さんでした。蜂すずめは花の蜜をたべ、かわせみはお魚を食べ、夜だかは羽虫をとってたべるのでした。それによだかには、するどい爪もするどいくちばしもありませんでしたから、どんなに弱い鳥でも、よだかをこわがる筈はなかったのです。

This being the case, it might seem odd that there is a "hawk" in the nighthawk's name. Yet, for one thing, the nighthawk's wings are uncannily strong, and when he soars, cutting the wind, he looks just like a hawk. For another, his cry pierces the sky. So it's not so odd, after all, that he's called a hawk.

Now, it goes without saying that the hawk didn't let this pass it by. In fact, it didn't like it one bit. And because of this, whenever it caught sight of the nighthawk, it peered at him, bristled up its shoulders and said, "You dump that name and get yourself a new one!"

One evening, the hawk finally went to the nighthawk's house.

"Hey, you in there? Still have the same old name, do ya? You've got a lot of nerve, you shameless little bird. You and I aren't birds of a feather, you know. Take me. I can fly through the blue sky to the ends of the earth. Now, take you. You only come out at night or on some dim cloudy day. Now take a good look at my beak and talons and compare them with your own, and you'll see what I mean."

"Mr. Hawk. It's asking too much of me to change my name. I had no hand in getting it in the first place. It came to me from heaven."

"Whadda ya talkin' about, eh? You could say that I got my name from heaven, but your name is just borrowed from mine and the night's. Now, give it back!"

"Mr. Hawk. It's beyond me to do that."

それなら、たかという名のついたことは不思議なようですが、これは、一つはよだかのはねが無暗（むやみ）に強くて、風を切って翔（か）けるときなどは、まるで鷹（たか）のように見えたことと、も一つはなきごえがするどくて、やはりどこか鷹に似ていた為（ため）です。もちろん、鷹は、これをひじょうに気にかけて、いやがっていました。それですから、よだかの顔さえ見ると、肩をいからせて、早く名前をあらためろ、名前をあらためろと、いうのでした。

　ある夕方、とうとう、鷹がよだかのうちへやって参りました。

「おい。居るかい。まだお前は名前をかえないのか。ずいぶんお前も恥知らずだな。お前とおれでは、よっぽど人格がちがうんだよ。たとえばおれは、青いそらをどこまででも飛んで行く。おまえは、曇ってうすぐらい日か、夜でなくちゃ、出て来ない。それから、おれのくちばしやつめを見ろ。そして、よくお前のとくらべて見るがいい。」

「鷹さん。それはあんまり無理です。私の名前は私が勝手につけたのではありません。神さまから下さったのです。」

「いいや。おれの名なら、神さまから貰（もら）ったのだと言ってもよかろうが、お前のは、言わば、おれと夜と、両方から借りてあるんだ。さあ返せ。」

「鷹さん。それは無理です。」

this being the case 「それなら」、そういう訳だから

uncannily 「無暗に」、異常に、不気味なほどに

for another 「も一つは」、もう１つ、さらに

it goes without saying 「もちろん」、言うまでもなく

didn't let this pass it by 「これをひじょうに気にかけて」、これを見過ごさなかった

bristled up its shoulders 「肩をいからせて」

dump that name 「名前をあらためろ」、その名を捨てろ

You've got a lot of nerve. 「ずいぶんお前は恥知らずだな」、ずうずうしい

aren't birds of a feather 「よっぽど人格がちがうんだよ」、同じ穴のムジナじゃない

talons （タカやワシなどの）爪

I had no hand in getting it in the first place. 「私の名前は私が勝手につけたのではありません」（had no hand in...: 〜には手を出さなかった、〜に関わっていなかった）

Whadda ya talkin' about? 「いいや」、何を言っているんだ。What are you talking about? の口語体

it's beyond me to do that 「それは無理」、そうするのは私の能力を超えている

"Beyond you? Rubbish. I'll give you a nice name, okay? You'll be called Ichizo. Ichizo, got it? Pretty good name, eh? And, when you change your name, you've got to make an official name-changing announcement. Okay? So, listen. You're gonna hang a name tag with ICHIZO written on it around your neck. Then you're gonna go around bowing to all the birds where they live and announce yourself by saying, From now on, I shall be known as Ichizo."

"There's no way in the world I could do that."

"Rubbish. You can. And you will. If you haven't done it by the morning of the day after tomorrow, I'll rip you to shreds with my talons before you know what's hit you. Keep that in mind, being clawed to death. On the morning of the day after tomorrow, I will go around from one bird's place to another and ask if you've been there or not. If there's even a single place you haven't been to, consider yourself dead as a dodo."

"But … don't you think that's a bit overdoing it? I'd rather die than have to do all that. Please do away with me right now."

"Well, why don't you sleep on it, okay? I mean, what's so bad about Ichizo, eh? Sounds like a pretty good name to me."

The hawk spread its wings fully out and flew back home to its nest.

The nighthawk shut his eyes, plunged in thought.

"Why on earth does everybody hate me like this so much? It's because I look like I have miso splattered over my face and my beak is split up to my ears. But I've never ever done a bad thing to anybody. When the little baby white-eye fell from its nest, I saved it and took it back. And the white-eye tore the chick right away from me as if it was taking it back from some kind of robber or something. And then it just cackled right in my face. And now I have to go around hanging a tag around my neck saying my name's Ichizo. That's the last straw, if you ask me."

「無理じゃない。おれがいい名を教えてやろう。市蔵というんだ。市蔵とな。いい名だろう。そこで、名前を変えるには、改名の披露というものをしないといけない。いいか。それはな、首へ市蔵と書いたふだをぶらさげて、私は以来市蔵と申しますと、口上を言って、みんなの所をおじぎしてまわるのだ。」

「そんなことはとても出来ません。」

「いいや。出来る。そうしろ。もしあさっての朝までに、お前がそうしなかったら、もうすぐ、つかみ殺すぞ。つかみ殺してしまうから、そう思え。おれはあさっての朝早く、鳥のうちを一軒ずつまわって、お前が来たかどうかを聞いてあるく。一軒でも来なかったという家があったら、もう貴様もその時がおしまいだぞ。」

「だってそれはあんまり無理じゃありませんか。そんなことをする位なら、私はもう死んだ方がましです。今すぐ殺して下さい。」

「まあ、よく、あとで考えてごらん。市蔵なんてそんなにわるい名じゃないよ。」鷹は大きなはねを一杯にひろげて、自分の巣の方へ飛んで帰って行きました。

よだかは、じっと目をつぶって考えました。

（一たい僕は、なぜこうみんなにいやがられるのだろう。僕の顔は、味噌をつけたようで、口は裂けてるからなあ。それだって、僕は今まで、なんにも悪いことをしたことがない。赤ん坊のめじろが巣から落ちていたときは、助けて巣へ連れて行ってやった。そしたらめじろは、赤ん坊をまるでぬす人からでもとりかえすように僕からひきはなしたんだなあ。それからひどく僕を笑ったっけ。それにああ、今度は市蔵だなんて、首へふだをかけるなんて、つらいはなしだなあ。）

Rubbish. ばかばかしい

official name-changing announcement 「改名の披露」、名称変更の正式発表

being clawed to death 「つかみ殺して」、爪で引き裂かれて死ぬ

dead as a dodo 「おしまい」、完全に死んでいる。dodo は絶滅した大型の鳥

don't you think that's a bit overdoing it? 「それはあんまり無理じゃありませんか」（overdoing...: 〜をやりすぎる）

do away with me 「私はもう死んだ方がまし」、私を殺してくれ

sleep on it 「あとで考えて」、一晩寝かせて考えて

plunged in thought 「考えました」、物思いにふけった

white-eye 「めじろ」

cackled right in my face 「ひどく僕を笑った」、面と向かって私をゲラゲラ笑った

the last straw 「つらいはなし」、我慢の限界

The day turned dim and gloomy as the nighthawk alighted from his nest and flew off into the low-lying clouds. He flew about the sky without making a sound, scraping clouds that glowed with a menacing light.

Then suddenly the nighthawk opened his mouth wide, stretched his wings straight as straight can be, and shot across the sky like an arrow. Bird louse after bird louse flowed into his throat. No sooner was he about to plunge into the earth than did he spring easily right up back to the sky. The clouds had turned all gray, and the distant mountains were a fiery red.

When the nighthawk took to flying like that, it seemed like the very sky was split in two. A beetle who got caught in his throat started to wriggle and writhe for dear life. The nighthawk swallowed the beetle right down, but for some reason soon felt shivers up and down his spine.

The clouds were now pitch black, reflecting the fiery red of the mountains just in the east. It was terrifying. The nighthawk set out once again for the sky, choked with emotion.

Just then one more beetle got into his throat, flapping away as if bent on scratching it from the inside. The nighthawk forced the beetle down, but this just choked him up all the more; and he wept, crying out at the top of his lungs. And as he wept, he circled round and round and round the sky.

"Ah, little beetle, every night I kill many bird lice. Now the hawk is going to kill me, and there's just one of me. It's so hard to swallow. Ah, I can't take it. I can't cope any longer. I'm going to stop eating insects and starve to death. But, before that, the hawk will probably do away with me. But, before that, I'm going to go far and far away, beyond the sky."

あたりは、もううすくらくなっていました。夜だかは巣から飛び出しました。雲が意地悪く光って、低くたれています。夜だかはまるで雲とすれすれになって、音なく空を飛びまわりました。

それからにわかによだかは口を大きくひらいて、はねをまっすぐに張って、まるで矢のようにそらをよこぎりました。小さな羽虫が幾匹も幾匹もその咽喉<ruby>咽喉<rt>のど</rt></ruby>にはいりました。

からだがつちにつくかつかないうちに、よだかはひらりとまたそらへはねあがりました。もう雲は<ruby>鼠色<rt>ねずみいろ</rt></ruby>になり、向うの山には山焼けの火がまっ赤です。

夜だかが思い切って飛ぶときは、そらがまるで二つに切れたように思われます。一<ruby>疋<rt>びき</rt></ruby>の<ruby>甲虫<rt>かぶとむし</rt></ruby>が、夜だかの咽喉にはいって、ひどくもがきました。よだかはすぐそれを呑<ruby>呑<rt>の</rt></ruby>みこみましたが、その時何だかせなかがぞっとしたように思いました。

雲はもうまっくろく、東の方だけ山やけの火が赤くうつって、恐ろしいようです。よだかはむねがつかえたように思いながら、またそらへのぼりました。

また一疋の甲虫が、夜だかののどに、はいりました。そしてまるでよだかの咽喉をひっかいてばたばたしました。よだかはそれを無理にのみこんでしまいましたが、その時、急に胸がどきっとして、夜だかは大声をあげて泣き出しました。泣きながらぐるぐるぐるぐる空をめぐったのです。

（ああ、かぶとむしや、たくさんの羽虫が、毎晩僕に殺される。そしてそのただ一つの僕がこんどは鷹に殺される。それがこんなにつらいのだ。ああ、つらい、つらい。僕はもう虫をたべないで<ruby>餓<rt>う</rt></ruby>えて死のう。いやその前にもう鷹が僕を殺すだろう。いや、その前に、僕は遠くの遠くの空の向うに行ってしまおう。）

alighted from... 「〜から飛び出しました」、〜から降りた

wriggle and writhe for dear life 「ひどくもがきました」、命がけでもがいた

It's so hard to swallow. 「それがこんなにつらいのだ」、それは受け入れがたい

can't cope any longer 「ああ、つらい、つらい」、もう耐えられない

The flames of light on the mountains gradually spread, flowing like water through the clouds and lighting them a fiery red.

The nighthawk made a beeline for the home of his little brother, the kingfisher. The lovely kingfisher had just awakened and was gazing at the flames of light on the distant mountains.

"Good evening, big brother," he said, watching the nighthawk descend. "What brings you here out of the blue?"

"Uh, it's just that I'm on my way to a faraway place. I came to see you before, that's all."

"No, you can't go! The hummingbird is already so far away, and I'll be left all by myself."

"Well, yeah. You see, there's nothing I can do about that. Just let things be. And, by the way, from now on, I don't want you taking any fish just for fun. Only when you really need to. Well, goodbye now."

"What's the matter? No, just wait a little bit longer."

"No, there's no difference whether I go now or later. Please don't forget to remember me to the hummingbird. Goodbye. We won't meet again. Goodbye now."

The nighthawk wept as he returned to his home. The short summer night was already coming to an end. Fern fronds swayed in the cold blue light, sucking in the dawn mist. The nighthawk cried out in a high-pitched screech, then, having put his nest in order and having properly preened all his feathers, once again flew away.

The mist lifted, and the sun rose exactly from the east. The nighthawk flew straight toward it like an arrow, wobbling in the air from the blinding light.

山焼けの火は、だんだん水のように流れてひろがり、雲も赤く燃えているようです。

よだかはまっすぐに、弟の川せみの所へ飛んで行きました。きれいな川せみも、丁度起きて遠くの山火事を見ていた所でした。そしてよだかの降りて来たのを見て言いました。

「兄さん。今晩は。何か急のご用ですか。」

「いいや、僕は今度遠い所へ行くからね、その前ちょっとお前に遭いに来たよ。」

「兄さん。行っちゃいけませんよ。蜂雀（はちすずめ）もあんな遠くにいるんですし、僕ひとりぼっちになってしまうじゃありませんか。」

「それはね。どうも仕方ないのだ。もう今日は何も言わないでくれ。そしてお前もね、どうしてもとらなければならない時のほかはいたずらにお魚を取ったりしないようにしてくれ。ね、さよなら。」

「兄さん。どうしたんです。まあもうちょっとお待ちなさい。」

「いや、いつまで居てもおんなじだ。はちすずめへ、あとでよろしく言ってやってくれ。さよなら。もうあわないよ。さよなら。」

よだかは泣きながら自分のお家へ帰って参りました。みじかい夏の夜はもうあけかかっていました。

羊歯（しだ）の葉は、よあけの霧を吸って、青くつめたくゆれました。よだかは高くきしきしきしと鳴きました。そして巣の中をきちんとかたづけ、きれいにからだ中のはねや毛をそろえて、また巣から飛び出しました。

霧がはれて、お日さまが丁度東からのぼりました。よだかはぐらぐらするほどまぶしいのをこらえて、矢のように、そっちへ飛んで行きました。

---

made a beeline for...
「まっすぐに〜へ飛んで行きました」

out of the blue 「急の」、だしぬけに

Just let things be. 「何も言わないでくれ」、事態を自然の成り行きに任して

remember me to... 「〜へ、よろしく云ってやってくれ」

fern fronds 「羊歯の葉」

properly preened all his feathers 「きれいにからだ中のはねや毛をそろえて」、すべての羽をきれいに整え（preen: 毛づくろいをする）

the mist lifted 「霧がはれて」

wobbling 「ぐらぐらする」

"Oh, Sun, Mr. Sun. Please take me to you. I don't mind if I die in flames. Even an ugly body like mine will give off a little light when it burns. I beg you, please take me to you."

But no matter how far he flew, the nighthawk got no closer to the sun. On the contrary, the sun seemed to be getting farther and farther away.

"You're the nighthawk, aren't you," said the sun. "I see. It must be pretty hard for you. Now, go and fly around the sky and ask the same thing of the stars. When you come down to it, you're not a daylight bird."

The nighthawk gave a bow and, in a flash, spiraled down onto the grass of a meadow. What happened after that was like out of a dream. His body was streaming high up amongst red and yellow stars, taken by the wind for what seemed like forever, as if the hawk had come and was gripping him in its talons.

Without warning, something cold fell on the nighthawk's face, and he opened his eyes. Dew was dripping from a single young stalk of pampas grass. Night had fallen, the air was giving off a pale light, and stars were twinkling from one horizon to the other. The nighthawk took off for the sky. As before, the fiery mountains were a brilliant red. The nighthawk flew amidst the dim reflection coming off the fiery-red mountains and the cold light of the stars. It flew once around the sky again, then set its sights straight for the beautiful stars of Orion in the western sky, calling out as it flew toward them.

"Oh, Stars, pale stars of the West. Please, I beg you, take me to you. I don't mind if I die in flames."

「お日さん、お日さん。どうぞ私をあなたの所へ連れてって下さい。灼けて死んでもかまいません。私のようなみにくいからだでも灼けるときには小さなひかりを出すでしょう。どうか私を連れてって下さい。」

　行っても行っても、お日さまは近くなりませんでした。かえってだんだん小さく遠くなりながらお日さまが言いました。

「お前はよだかだな。なるほど、ずいぶんつらかろう。今度そらを飛んで、星にそうたのんでごらん。お前はひるの鳥ではないのだからな。」

　夜だかはおじぎを一つしたと思いましたが、急にぐらぐらしてとうとう野原の草の上に落ちてしまいました。そしてまるで夢を見ているようでした。からだがずうっと赤や黄の星のあいだをのぼって行ったり、どこまでも風に飛ばされたり、また鷹が来てからだをつかんだりしたようでした。

　つめたいものがにわかに顔に落ちました。よだかは眼をひらきました。一本の若いすすきの葉から露がしたたったのでした。もうすっかり夜になって、空は青ぐろく、一面の星がまたたいていました。よだかはそらへ飛びあがりました。今夜も山やけの火はまっかです。よだかはその火のかすかな照りと、つめたいほしあかりの中をとびめぐりました。それからもう一ぺん飛びめぐりました。そして思い切って西のそらのあの美しいオリオンの星の方に、まっすぐに飛びながら叫びました。

「お星さん。西の青じろいお星さん。どうか私をあなたのところへ連れてって下さい。灼けて死んでもかまいません。」

when you come down to it　要するに、結局のところ

in a flash　「急に」、一瞬で

spiraled down onto...　「ぐらぐらして～に落ちてしまいました」、螺旋状に～に落ちた

without warning　「にわかに」、前触れもなく

young stalk of pampas grass　「若いすすきの葉」、ススキの若い茎

stars of Orion　「オリオンの星」、オリオン座の星

Orion the Hunter gave the nighthawk the cold shoulder, not interrupting his brave old song. The nighthawk got all teary and tottered down, until he got ahold of himself and started to fly around the sky again. He then flew in a straight line for the Great Dog Star in the south, crying into the night.

"Oh, Star, great blue star of the South. Please, I beg you, take me to you. I don't mind if I die in flames."

"Come off it, will ya?" said the Great Dog, twinkling and blinking its beautiful stars in blues and purples and yellows. "Who on earth do you think you are anyway? Just a birdbrain, that's what. It would take you billions and trillions and zillions of years to reach here on those wings of yours."

And having said that, the Great Dog Star turned its back on him.

The nighthawk spiraled down, crestfallen, until he once again circled the sky, now aiming straight for the Great Bear in the north, crying out as he flew.

"Oh, Great Bear, blue star of the North. Please take me to you."

"You must have your head in the clouds," said the Great Bear in a laid-back way. "I think you better cool off that head of yours. Now, there's nothing like plunging into a sea floating with icebergs to get your head cooled off. And if there's no sea in the vicinity, diving into a glass of ice water will do the trick just fine."

This sent the nighthawk, dejected once again, into a tailspin, until he started to fly round and round the sky once more. Now he set out for the Eagle on the far bank of the Milky Way that had just begun to rise in the east.

"Oh, Eagle, white star of the East," he cried. "I beg of you, please take me to you. I don't mind if I die in flames."

オリオンは勇ましい歌をつづけながらよだかなどはてんで相手にしませんでした。よだかは泣きそうになって、よろよろと落ちて、それからやっとふみとまって、もう一ぺんとびめぐりました。それから、南の大犬座の方へまっすぐに飛びながら叫びました。

「お星さん。南の青いお星さん。どうか私をあなたの所へつれてって下さい。やけて死んでもかまいません。」

大犬は青や紫や黄やうつくしくせわしくまたたきながら言いました。

「馬鹿（ばか）を言うな。おまえなんか一体どんなものだい。たかが鳥じゃないか。おまえのはねでここまで来るには、億年兆年億兆年だ。」そしてまた別の方を向きました。

よだかはがっかりして、よろよろ落ちて、それからまた二へん飛びめぐりました。それからまた思い切って北の大熊星（おおぐまぼし）の方へまっすぐに飛びながら叫びました。

「北の青いお星さま、あなたの所へどうか私を連れてって下さい。」

大熊星はしずかに言いました。

「余計なことを考えるものではない。少し頭をひやして来なさい。そう言うときは、氷山の浮いている海の中へ飛び込むか、近くに海がなかったら、氷をうかべたコップの水の中へ飛び込むのが一等だ。」

よだかはがっかりして、よろよろ落ちて、それからまた、四へんそらをめぐりました。そしてもう一度、東から今のぼった天の川の向う岸の鷲（わし）の星に叫びました。

「東の白いお星さま、どうか私をあなたの所へ連れてって下さい。やけて死んでもかまいません。」

---

gave... the cold shoulder 「〜はてんで相手にしませんでした」、〜に冷たい態度を取った

got ahold of himself 「ふみとまって」、気を確かにして

Great Dog Star 「大犬座」、シリウス

Come off it, will ya? 「馬鹿を言うな」

just a birdbrain 「たかが鳥」（birdbrain: 愚か者、間抜け）

crestfallen 「がっかりして」、意気消沈して

Great Bear 「大熊星」

have your head in the clouds 「余計なことを考える」、雲の中に頭を突っ込んでいるように、現実を見ていない

in a laid-back way 「しずかに」、落ち着いて

do the trick just fine 「一等だ」、うまくいく、効果がある

dejected 「がっかりして」、すっかり落ち込んで

sent... into a tailspin 「よろよろ落ちて」

Eagle on the far bank of the Milky Way 「天の川の向う岸の鷲の星」

"Stop pulling my leg," bellowed the Eagle, arrogantly. "Not on your life. To be a star, you must have the appropriate status, not to mention a considerable amount of money."

This took the wind right out of the nighthawk's wings, which closed on him and sent him sailing downward. His frail legs were no more than a foot from the ground when he rocketed up like a flare. When he had reached a place near the middle of the sky, he gave his body a shake and bristled up his feathers, just like an eagle does when attacking a bear. He then cried out in the highest piercing pitch. He sounded just like a hawk. All of the birds asleep in the meadows and forests woke up and, quailing and quaking, looked up to the starry sky, wondering what in heaven's name could be behind that sound.

The nighthawk flew on forever and ever, straight up into the sky. The fiery-red mountains were now no bigger than the tip of a cigarette. The nighthawk just climbed and climbed and climbed.

鷲は大風に言いました。

「いいや、とてもとても、話にも何にもならん。星になるには、それ相応の身分でなくちゃいかん。またよほど金もいるのだ。」

よだかはもうすっかり力を落してしまって、はねを閉じて、地に落ちて行きました。そしてもう一尺で地面にその弱い足がつくというとき、よだかは俄かにのろしのようにそらへとびあがりました。そらのなかほどへ来て、よだかはまるで鷲が熊を襲うときするように、ぶるっとからだをゆすって毛をさかだてました。

それからキシキシキシキシキシキシッと高く高く叫びました。その声はまるで鷹でした。野原や林にねむっていたほかのとりは、みんな目をさまして、ぶるぶるふるえながら、いぶかしそうにほしぞらを見あげました。

夜だかは、どこまでも、どこまでも、まっすぐに空へのぼって行きました。もう山焼けの火はたばこの吸殻のくらいにしか見えません。よだかはのぼってのぼって行きました。

pulling my leg　からかう、ひやかす

Not on your life. 「話にも何にもならん」、とんでもない

appropriate status
「それ相応の身分」

a foot 「一尺」。尺は長さの単位で一尺約30cm

bristled up his feathers 「毛をさかだてました」

quailing and quaking
「ぶるぶるふるえながら」

His breath froze white on his chest from the cold. And because the air was getting thinner and thinner, he had to flap his wings all the more. And yet, the stars looked no bigger than they did before. Each breath went in and out like the air in bellows. The cold and frost stabbed into him like little swords, and his wings became numb all over. He then looked up at the sky with tears in his eyes.

This was his final moment. Whether he was falling at that moment or climbing, whether upside down or right side up, he couldn't tell. But for all that, his heart was at ease, and his big bloodstained beak was bent to one side, clearly in a little smile.

It wasn't long after that that the nighthawk opened his eyes wide and saw that his body was burning quietly, giving off an exquisite phosphorescent blue light. Beside him sat Cassiopeia, and just in back of him flowed the pale light of the Milky Way.

The Nighthawk Star didn't stop burning. It continued to burn on and on and on. It burns like that to this very day.

寒さにいきはむねに白く凍りました。空気がうすくなった為に、はねをそれはそれはせわしくうごかさなければなりませんでした。

　それだのに、ほしの大きさは、さっきと少しも変りません。つくいきはふいごのようです。寒さや霜がまるで剣のようによだかを刺しました。よだかははねがすっかりしびれてしまいました。そしてなみだぐんだ目をあげてもう一ぺんそらを見ました。そうです。これがよだかの最後でした。もうよだかは落ちているのか、のぼっているのか、さかさになっているのか、上を向いているのかも、わかりませんでした。ただこころもちはやすらかに、その血のついた大きなくちばしは、横にまがっては居ましたが、たしかに少しわらって居りました。

　それからしばらくたってよだかははっきりまなこをひらきました。そして自分のからだがいま燐の火のような青い美しい光になって、しずかに燃えているのを見ました。

　すぐとなりは、カシオピア座でした。天の川の青じろいひかりが、すぐうしろになっていました。

　そしてよだかの星は燃えつづけました。いつまでもいつまでも燃えつづけました。

　今でもまだ燃えています。

bellows 「ふいご」

his heart was at ease
「こころもちはやすらか」、
心は安らかだった

phosphorescent blue
light 「青じろいひかり」

Cassiopeia 「カシオピ
ア座」

永訣の朝
The Morning of Last Farewell

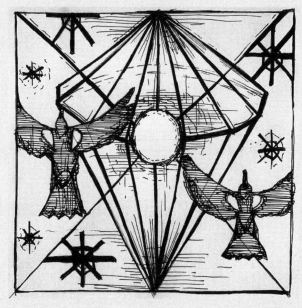

イラスト：ルーシー・パルバース

The Morning of Last Farewell を読むまえに

天上のアイスクリーム

最愛の妹トシとの、この世における最期の別れの時が刻々と迫る。その時を迎えようとする中で、賢治は深い悲しみと慟哭の果てに何を見るのか。賢治はその覚悟をこの詩に託す。

🔊 **11** *p.180*

　「永訣の朝」は、賢治の最も親密な親愛の情を表した詩と言えるかもしれません。両親を除けば、妹のトシとの関係は、彼の人生において最も大切なものであり、トシの死は、その中でも最も重大な出来事だったからです。

　賢治とトシとの年齢差はわずか2歳。1922年11月27日、24歳の誕生日を迎えて2週間ほどでトシが亡くなったとき、賢治は愛しい妹の末期の水を取っていました。トシは、「羅須地人協会」と呼ばれることになる別宅で何日か床に伏したあと、11月19日、実家に移り、その8日後の27日に亡くなったのです。トシが息をひきとったとき、賢治は押入れに頭を突っ込んで泣きました。

　冒頭の4行、

　けふのうちに

　とほくへいってしまうわたくしのいもうとよ

　みぞれがふっておもてはへんにあかるいのだ

　（＊あめゆじゆとてちてけんじや）

はすべてひらがなで書かれており、この詩の叙情的で悲しげなトーンを作り出しています。特に4行目の「あめゆじゆとてちてけんじや」は心に強く響きます。これは、ふたりが子どもの頃に共有した地元の方言です。この「けんじや」いう言葉は、「お願い」という意味と、トシの兄の名前である「賢治」という意味の両方があります。

　賢治は「陰惨な」雲から「びちよびちよ」降り注ぐみぞれをお椀

で受けるために外に出ました。日本語の「陰惨な」は 英語では、gruesome や sorrowful などいろいろな訳し方がありますが、私は、同じ母音の音にしようと考えて "cruel and gloomy" としました。また、gloomy は gl で始まる擬態語で、「光」、この場合は「その不在」を意味します。sloshing も日本語の「びちょびちょ」を模した擬声語です。

　賢治は妹の熱を雪で冷まそうとします。彼は雪をトシの額に当てたり、口に入れたりします。

　賢治は雪について、「この雪はどこをえらぼうにも／あんまりどこもまつしろなのだ」と言っています。これは、雪を生み出す極楽浄土自体の純度の高さを示しています。賢治にとって、風、雨、雪といった要素は、あの世からのメッセージを伝えるものです。雪は天国から地球に降ってくるアイスクリームなのです。トシがこの世よりも遥かに素晴らしく美しい場所に行くという、賢治の確固たる信念を示しています。

　終盤の3行、

　うまれでくるたて

　こんどはこたにわりやのごとばかりで

　くるしまなあようにうまれてくる

　も、すべてひらがなで書かれており、自らの信念への確信が語られ
ています。賢治の望みは、自分が死んだら、この世に戻る必要のない
場所に行くことです。賢治はこの言葉の中で、たとえ生まれ変わった
としても、人の苦しみを自分の負担として背負い、大らかで無私無欲
な精神を持って生まれ変わるのだと語っています。

　このことは彼の切なる願いです。来世、あるいはその次の世、その
また次の世で、自分を「クニサレズ」、すべての人の病気だの悩みだの
苦しみなどを自分のものとして引き受けることができるようになりた
い、という願いです。

　ここに、宮沢賢治の思い、希望、願望の真髄が見えてきます。

The Morning of Last Farewell

O my little sister
Who will travel far on this day
It is sleeting outside and strangely light
  (fetch me the rainlike snow)
The sleet sloshing down
Out of pale red clouds cruel and gloomy
  (fetch me the rainlike snow)
I shot out into the midst of this black sleet
A bent bullet
To gather the rainlike snow for you to eat
In two chipped ceramic bowls
Decorated with blue watershields
  (fetch me the rainlike snow)
The sleet sloshes down, sinking
Out of somber clouds the color of bismuth
O Toshiko
You asked me for a bowl
Of this refreshing snow
When you were on the point of death
To brighten my life forever
Thank you my brave little sister
I too will not waver from my path
  (fetch me the rainlike snow)
You made your request to me
Amidst gasping and the intensest fever
For the last bowl of snow given off
By the world of the sky called the atmosphere the galaxy and
  sun

永訣の朝

けふのうちに
とほくへいつてしまふわたくしのいもうとよ
みぞれがふつておもてはへんにあかるいのだ
　　　　（＊あめゆじゆとてちてけんじや）
うすあかくいつそう陰惨な雲から
みぞれはびちよびちよふつてくる
　　　　（あめゆじゆとてちてけんじや）
青い蓴菜のもやうのついた
これらふたつのかけた陶椀に
おまへがたべるあめゆきをとらうとして
わたくしはまがつたてつぱうだまのやうに
このくらいみぞれのなかに飛びだした
　　　　（あめゆじゆとてちてけんじや）
蒼鉛いろの暗い雲から
みぞれはびちよびちよ沈んでくる
ああとし子
死ぬといふいまごろになつて
わたくしをいつしやうあかるくするために
こんなさつぱりした雪のひとわんを
おまへはわたくしにたのんだのだ
ありがたうわたくしのけなげないもうとよ
わたくしもまつすぐにすすんでいくから
　　　　（あめゆじゆとてちてけんじや）
はげしいはげしい熱やあへぎのあひだから
おまへはわたくしにたのんだのだ
　銀河や太陽　気圏などとよばれたせかいの
そらからおちた雪のさいごのひとわんを……

last farewell 「永訣」、永遠の別れ

rainlike snow 「あめゆじ」、雨のような雪、みぞれ

sloshing down 「びちよびちよふつてくる」、バシャバシャ降ってくる

shot out into... 「〜のなかに飛びだした」

a bent bullet 「まがつたてつぱうだま」

watershields 「蓴菜」、ジュンサイ。スイレン科の水草

somber clouds 「暗い雲」、薄暗い雲

bismuth 「蒼鉛」

not waver from my path 「まつすぐにすすんでいく」、自分の道からそれない

atmosphere 「気圏」、大気圏

galaxy 「銀河」

The sleet, desolate, collects
On two large fragments of granite blocks
I'll stand precariously on them
And fetch the last morsels of food
For my sweet and tender sister
Off this lustrous pine branch
Covered in transparent cold droplets
Holding the purewhite dual properties of water and snow
Now today you will part forever
With the deepblue pattern on these bowls
So familiar to us as we grew up together
(I go as I go by myself)
You are truly bidding farewell on this day
O my brave little sister
Burning up pale white and gentle
In the dark screens and mosquito net
Of your stifling sickroom
This snow is so white everywhere
No matter where you take it from
This exquisite snow has come
From such a terrifying and disarranged sky
  (when I am born again
  I will be born to suffer
  Not only on my own account)
I now will pray with all my heart
That the snow you will eat from these two bowls
Will be transformed into heaven's icecream
And be offered to you and everyone as material that will be holy
On this wish I stake my every happiness

desolate 「さびしく」、陰鬱な

two large fragments of granite blocks 「ふたきれのみかげせきざい」。御影石材とは、花崗岩の建築用石材でお墓などにも使用される

precariously 「あぶなく」、危なっかしく

the last morsels of food 「さいごのたべもの」、最後の一口の食べ物

dual properties 「二相系」。異なる２つの相が共存している状態。ここでは雪と水が共存しそれぞれになっている

I go as I go by myself 「Ora Orade Shitori egumo」、私は私で一人で逝きます

bidding farewell 「わかれてしまふ」、別れを告げる

screens 「びやうぶ」、屏風

mosquito net 「かや」

stifling sickroom 「とざされた病室」、息苦しい病室

exquisite snow 「うつくしい雪」、この上なく美しい雪

terrifying and disarranged sky 「おそろしいみだれたそら」

only on my own account 「わりやのごとばかりで」、自分で、自分の力で

……ふたきれのみかげせきざいに
みぞれはさびしくたまつてゐる
わたくしはそのうへにあぶなくたち
雪と水とのまつしろな二相系(にさうけい)をたもち
すきとほるつめたい雫にみちた
このつややかな松のえだから
わたくしのやさしいいもうとの
さいごのたべものをもらつていかう
わたしたちがいつしよにそだつてきたあひだ
みなれたちやわんのこの藍のもやうにも
もうけふおまへはわかれてしまふ
　（＊Ora Orade Shitori egumo）
ほんたうにけふおまへはわかれてしまふ
あああのとざされた病室の
くらいびやうぶやかやのなかに
やさしくあをじろく燃えてゐる
わたくしのけなげないもうとよ
この雪はどこをえらばうにも
あんまりどこもまつしろなのだ
あんなおそろしいみだれたそらから
このうつくしい雪がきたのだ
　　　（＊うまれでくるたて
　　　　こんどはこたにわりやのごとばかりで
　　　　くるしまなあよにうまれてくる）
おまへがたべるこのふたわんのゆきに
わたくしはいまこころからいのる
どうかこれが天上のアイスクリームになつて
おまへとみんなとに聖い資糧をもたらすやうに
わたくしのすべてのさいはひをかけてねがふ

ロジャー・パルバース
Roger Pulvers

　作家、劇作家、演出家、翻訳家、映画監督、東京工業大学名誉教授。1944年、ニューヨークで生まれる。カリフォルニア大学ロサンゼルス校、ハーバード大学大学院卒業。ベトナム戦争への反発からアメリカを離れ、ワルシャワ、パリに留学ののち、1967年に初来日し、京都産業大学、東京工業大学で教鞭をとる。現在はオーストラリア在住。日本に度々帰国している。

　著書には、『星砂物語』（小説：講談社）、『ぼくがアメリカ人をやめたワケ』（大沢章子訳　集英社インターナショナル）、『驚くべき日本語』（早川敦子訳　集英社インターナショナル）など多数。

　宮沢賢治の翻訳・研究者としても知られ、『英語で読む銀河鉄道の夜』（ちくま文庫）、『賢治から、あなたへ　世界はすべてつながっている』（森本奈理訳　集英社インターナショナル）などの著書多数。『「銀河鉄道の夜」を英語で読む』、『「チェロ弾きのゴーシュ」「注文の多い料理店」を英語で読む』（コスモピア）などがある。

宮沢賢治 原文英訳シリーズ３

『風の又三郎』を英語で読む

2023年8月1日　第1版第1刷発行

英訳・解説：ロジャー・パルバース

編集協力：熊沢敏之、田中和也、大岩根麻衣、山口西夏

装丁：松本田鶴子

カバー写真：yspbqh14_AdobeStock
本文イラスト：ルーシー・パルバース

発行人：坂本由子
発行所：コスモピア株式会社
　　　　〒151-0053　東京都渋谷区代々木4-36-4　MCビル2F
営業部：TEL: 03-5302-8378　email: mas@cosmopier.com
編集部：TEL: 03-5302-8379　email: editorial@cosmopier.com

https://www.cosmopier.com/（コスモピア公式ホームページ）
https://e-st.cosmopier.com/（コスモピアeステーション）
https://kids-ebc.com/（子ども英語ブッククラブ）
印刷：シナノ印刷株式会社

本書へのご意見・ご感想をお聞かせください。

本書をお買い上げいただき、誠にありがとうございます。

今後の出版の参考にさせていただきたいので、ぜひ、ご意見・ご感想をお聞かせください。（PC またはスマートフォンで下記のアンケートフォームよりお願いいたします）

アンケートにご協力いただいた方の中から抽選で毎月 10 名の方に、コスモピア・オンラインショップ（https://www.cosmopier.net/）でお使いいただける 500 円のクーポンを差し上げます。（当選メールをもって発表にかえさせていただきます）

https://forms.gle/8sdiQsWegwZ81SCt6